Men and Women at Work

By

Katherine G. Kearney, Ph.D.
and Thomas I. White, Ph.D.

Men and Women at Work

By

Katherine G. Kearney, Ph.D.
and Thomas I. White, Ph.D.

CAREER PRESS
180 Fifth Avenue
P.O. Box 34
Hawthorne, NJ 07507
1-800-CAREER-1
201-427-0229 (outside U.S.)
FAX: 201-427-2037

MEN AND WOMEN AT WORK
ISBN 1-56414-132-2, $14.95
Cover design by The Gottry Communications Group, Inc.
Printed in the U.S.A. by Book-mart Press

To order this title by mail, please include price as noted above, $2.50 handling per order, and $1.00 for each book ordered. Send to: Career Press, Inc., 180 Fifth Ave., P.O. Box 34, Hawthorne, NJ 07507

Or call toll-free 1-800-CAREER-1 (Canada: 201-427-0229) to order using VISA or MasterCard, or for further information on books from Career Press.

Library of Congress Cataloging-in-Publication Data

Kearney, Katherine Grace.
    Men and women at work / by Katherine G. Kearney and Thomas White.
        p.   cm.
    Includes index.
    ISBN 1-56414-132-2 : $14.95
    1. Sex role in the work environment. 2. Communication--Sex differences. 3. Sex differences (Psychology) 4. Sexual harassment. I. White, Thomas, 1948-   II. Title.
    HD6060.6.K4   1994
    306.3'615--dc20   94-28292
                                                                              CIP

Dedication

To our families

Contents

Men and women at work

During the last 30 years, we have witnessed a series of confusing shifts in how men and women in our society have regarded the differences between themselves.

From the 1960s through the 1980s, the two sexes largely played down their differences. Gender differences had, after all, traditionally been used to justify discrimination against women. And the struggle for equal rights made us aware of the damage done by sexual stereotypes.

Once our culture got comfortable with the idea of sexual equality, however, people became fascinated with the differences between the sexes. The contrast in how men and women operated in business made it plain that the two sexes aren't the same, even though they are equal. And the best-selling books of Deborah Tannen and John Gray reminded us of how different we can be in personal relationships.

Yet as many of us studied these differences, it became increasingly apparent that they are not necessarily linked to sex. Many normal, emotionally healthy men think, talk, feel and work the way that gender experts claim that women do. And many women fit the "male" profile. Just when everyone thought they'd figured things out, it got harder again.

We've written this book to address these complexities. We wanted to write about the practical implications of the gender research for the workplace. But we also wanted to be sensitive to the sizable number of people who, when they hear generalizations about men and women, find themselves saying, "That's not me." Accordingly, we've chosen to discuss differences in how people operate at work mostly in terms of character type than sex. We believe that this gives us the best of both worlds. We describe two character types, "warriors" and "villagers," that correspond to dominant traits in most men and women, respectively. But talking about "warriors" and "villagers" instead of "men" and "women" insulates us from sex-role stereotyping. We believe that this approach gives people the insights necessary for successfully understanding and dealing with someone who, psychologically, lives in a different world. Yet it also derails an unfortunate human tendency to base conclusions about other people on irrelevant factors. We hope that you agree with this strategy.

This, like any book, was built with the help of many hands. We would like to thank our agent, Jeff Herman, and the staff of The Career Press. We would particularly like to acknowledge the generous assistance of the many people who either read early versions of the chapters or simply agreed to talk with us about the topic: Sam Bleecker, Kim Breese, Mary Beth Cheri, Betsy Hague, Harriet Lefkowith, Vicki Fuentes, Dee Pecoraro, Jan Sparrow, Kym Strempack, numerous friends, family members, colleagues and students. We are grateful to the members of various business groups and corporate workshops who were willing to be exposed to these ideas as we were still shaping them. And we especially appreciate the willingness of so many men and women in business to share private stories about their dealings with "warriors" and "villagers" on the job and their generosity in making suggestions for handling the problems that occur when the two types clash. For the sake of respecting individuals' privacy, we have modified all of the stories and scenarios described in the book. Virtually all of them, however, spring from someone's personal experience in the workplace.

Why you should read this book

Do any of these sound familiar?

- You are regularly baffled, frustrated, angered or nonplussed by members of the opposite sex with whom you work.

- Some people at work are easy to get along with. Others seem consistently foreign to you, even though you like them.

- You are, in your eyes, treated inexcusably by a co-worker. You confront that person. Yet he or she seems unable to understand why you are hurt or angry.

- You work hard, but you feel that you're regularly misunderstood by your co-workers or supervisor. No matter what you do, you feel that you and the people in your department never work well together. And you think this is also why you don't get the raises you think you deserve, and why you're always overlooked when it comes to promotions.

- You and your subordinates have, over time, learned to cooperate with each other. You have an efficient and pleasant way of working together. Then one day you have to work closely with another department on a project. That department works in a way completely different from yours. But you have to figure out some way to get the two groups to pull together.

- From everything you can tell, your boss is interested in you—in some way. But you don't know how to react. You wish you knew some way to figure out what's going on in his or her mind. And you need to know what to do.

If you, like most people, encounter situations like these, read on. This book addresses your concerns and helps you understand and deal with all of those "strange" people around you.

Chapter One

Bridging the gender gap in the workplace

One day a traveling salesman from the city went calling on clients in the country. Happy at being away from the city in which he lived and disarmed by the beauty of the land, Jay was soon cruising along contentedly. He was brought up short, however, as he headed up a hill and found a tractor coming over the crest in his lane. The other driver—Heather—quickly turned to avoid hitting Jay, but as she passed she looked right at him and yelled, "Pig! Pig! Pig!" Taken aback by the woman's words, Jay muttered some epithet under his breath and angrily gunned his car. As he sped over the hill, however, he was forced to slam on his brakes...in order to avoid crashing into a huge pig sitting in the middle of the road.

....

This old story is one that we should keep in mind as we explore the ever fascinating world of differences between men and women. Unquestioned assumptions about what a woman must mean when she yells "Pig!" at a man led Jay to misunderstand Heather's attempt to protect him—and the pig—from harm. And so it is with all of us if we automatically assume that the words or deeds of a man or woman mean exactly what we think they mean.

A growing body of research suggests that despite the egalitarian values of our culture and the progress of the women's movement over the last 30 years, men and women remain vastly different. Sociolinguist Deborah Tannen suggests that men and women speak different languages. Psychologist John Gray claims that they look for different things in personal relationships. Management experts Marilyn Loden and Judy Rosener argue that they prefer different management styles. And moral development psychologist Carol

Gilligan argues that they even think differently about right and wrong. Psychologist Gray claims that the differences between men and women are so great that we should probably see the two sexes as coming from different planets! To ignore such profound differences is to court disaster.

In this spirit, the tale of Heather, Jay and the pig is a perfect emblem for the difficulties men and women face when dealing with one another. As experts have claimed, men and women literally live in different worlds. Each world has its own view of what's important in life, and its own traditions about how people should deal with one another. However, while these traditions are readily understood by the natives of each world, they are just as readily misunderstood by outsiders. Any of Heather's neighbors would understand that calling out "Pig!" in such a situation was a friendly warning. Yet all of Jay's pals from the city would take Heather's shout as an unprovoked insult.

What to expect

This book is about how such basic differences between people surface in the workplace. We will help you understand these differences, and we'll give you practical suggestions for dealing with them—suggestions that may also be applicable to your personal life. We'll start with an overview of what experts have discovered about the fundamental psychological differences between men and women. We'll show how this affects the way the two sexes think about business. And we'll look at specific areas where difficulties arise in the workplace: working on "teams"; leading one another; inadvertently giving co-workers a hard time; and recognizing and handling sexual harassment. Our goal is to make it easier for you to get through your day at work without, we might say, misreading friendly warnings, unintentionally insulting someone, or needlessly putting yourself—or any livestock—at risk.

A few points to keep in mind

Before getting down to business, however, we want to offer a few important cautions.

1. *Different* does mean different. Take these differences seriously. That is, don't underestimate the differences between men's and women's outlooks and the two worlds they inhabit. And don't be lulled into thinking that we're looking only at superficial differences.

2. *Different* does not mean better or worse. Neither outlook is better or worse than the other. Jay lives in the city. Heather lives in the country. But it's no better to live in one place than the other. All of us automatically seem to assume that our way of thinking or doing things isn't simply one way, but the best way. But that's an assumption we must all give up if we want to live and work together.

We're going to be describing two very different outlooks in this book. Each has strengths. Each has weaknesses. But each is just as good as the other. You're going to be tempted to forget this and disparage the outlook opposite your own. Don't!

3. Gender: it is but it isn't. Although some researchers claim that the differences we're discussing spring from whether someone's male or female, we've discovered through interviewing many men and women for this book that the importance of gender is probably overstated. Some differences in psychology, preferred management style, and the like can be correlated to gender. Most male managers, for example, seem to prefer a leadership style based on authority, while most female managers seem more comfortable with building consensus. But this is true only *most* of the time. Regarding all of the traits that we'll talk about in this book, we've seen that a sizable minority of men and women always come up opposite from what many people would predict based solely on gender. So if you're part of that group, don't worry about it.

In fact, one of the most fascinating parts of writing this book was our discovery that there was so much "crossover" (that is, female warriors and male villagers)—and particularly among men. Over the last year, we administered the "warrior/villager" questionnaire in Chapter 1 to more than 250 people in business, largely in connection with corporate seminars. And even though this was far from a scientific survey, we think that the results are interesting enough to pass along.

The gender breakdown was nearly equal: 56 percent men, 44 percent women. Women came up largely what their sex would predict: 80 percent villagers and 20 percent warriors. Among the men, however, the percentages were different: 64 percent warriors and 36 percent villagers. This means that when all of the figures are combined, there may actually be more villagers—male and female—than warriors.

4. Not men and women, but warriors and villagers. The fact that predictions based on gender will so likely be wrong leads us to claim that the differences we see in one another spring more from different personality types than different genders. Accordingly, in this book, we're going to be talking about two very different views of the world, business, what's important in life and how you deal with people. We'll call one of these personality types the warrior and the other the villager. And we'll describe the differences.

At the same time, however, we aren't saying that gender is irrelevant. Most men at work turn out to be "warriors," and most women, "villagers." And on an issue like sexual harassment, gender is critical. This book is based on a large and growing body of research about fundamental personality differences that may or may not be linked to gender, but that nonetheless produce some powerful differences in how people operate in the workplace.

Don't forget the basics

We've learned through conducting numerous corporate workshops that it will be easier for you to recognize and work with people opposite from you if you first understand what experts have discovered in the last decade about some basic psychological differences between the sexes. Accordingly, we're going to begin with the basics. Heather and Jay would have dealt with one another more successfully if they'd known more about where the other one came from. So we're going to spend this chapter describing the major psychological differences that experts have found between men and women.

And remember just how profound these differences are as you try to understand one another on the job. We promise that as long as you keep the basics in mind, handling practical problems will be much easier. You'll understand better the motivations and customs of people very different from you. And when facing difficulties, you'll find it easier to create solutions that give everyone what they want.

A questionnaire

First, however, take a few minutes and answer the questionnaire on pages 20 and 21. Read each statement. Then check "yes" or "no" according to whether the sentence, for the most part, describes you.

Two sexes, two outlooks

For thousands of years, men and women have been grappling with the powerful differences between them. Sometimes we've glorified those differences. Sometimes we have denounced them. At different times in human history, one sex or the other has claimed a privileged status because of them. In the last 30 years we've tended to deny these differences, following our society's commitment to equality and to the idea that race, color, creed, sex or sexual orientation shouldn't determine where we live, work or go to school.

Yet despite our society's official position that there are no significant differences between men and women, all of us have continued to have bewildering experiences with the opposite sex. And despite everything we say publicly about the equality of the sexes, in our most private moments, most of us have been unable to shake the irrational fear that members of the opposite sex might actually be aliens from another galaxy who have assumed human form.

Research in the last 10 years, however, has concluded that these differences are real. Men and women may not be the "aliens" we feared they were. But they are different enough that the common term "the opposite

A questionnaire

1. I am comfortable asking people for help.

◇ Yes   ◇ No

2. I enjoy being the center of attention at meetings.

◇ Yes   ◇ No

3. When talking about myself, I tend to minimize my accomplishments.

◇ Yes   ◇ No

4. I enjoy playing practical jokes.   ◇ Yes   ◇ No

5. My feelings are easily hurt.   ◇ Yes   ◇ No

6. On the job, I am strategic and political in advancing my career.

◇ Yes   ◇ No

7. I tend to hold onto feelings of being hurt by other people, and I have trouble trusting someone who's hurt me.

◇ Yes   ◇ No

8. I'm comfortable competing openly against other people, and I like the feeling of beating someone else out of something—a promotion, raise, etc.

◇ Yes   ◇ No

9. I like having intimate conversations with friends about personal matters.

◇ Yes   ◇ No

10. I tend to interrupt other people in conversations.

◇ Yes   ◇ No

11. It's relatively easy for me to apologize to someone or to admit that I was wrong.

◇ Yes   ◇ No

12. I like to come up with funny or clever ways to "rib" friends or people I work with.

◇ Yes ◇ No

13. I enjoy talking about relationships and feelings.

◇ Yes ◇ No

14. I like to tell jokes. ◇ Yes ◇ No

15. If I meet some people as I'm walking in a hallway or on a sidewalk, I tend to walk around them.

◇ Yes ◇ No

16. In my dealings with people, I don't beat around the bush. I get right to the point, even if it means being blunt. ◇ Yes ◇ No

17. I take pains not to hurt other people's feelings by what I say to them.

◇ Yes ◇ No

18. I like giving orders. ◇ Yes ◇ No

19. I hate verbal confrontations. ◇ Yes ◇ No

20. I'm very ambitious for power, status and money.

◇ Yes ◇ No

21. If I have a personal problem, I like to talk to a close friend about it.

◇ Yes ◇ No

Now score the questionnaire as follows: In the odd-numbered questions, count each "yes" as a "V" and each "no" as a "W." In the even-numbered questions, count each "yes" as a "W" and each "no" as a "V." You will end up with two scores, a "W" score and a "V" score.

Put your scores aside for now, and we'll come back to them shortly.

sex" is surprisingly accurate. Researchers have discovered that most men and women have virtually opposite psychologies, seeing themselves and the world around them quite differently. In fact, the psychological differences are so powerful and deep-seated that it is best to think of men and women as living in *different worlds*.

In this way, then, our opening story about Heather and Jay is not far from the mark. However, trying to make the differences between men and women analogous to the differences between "city folk" and "country folk" isn't pushing it far enough. The research has shown that the differences between men and women are much more dramatic than that—something more akin to the differences between, let us say, *warriors* and *villagers*.

Warriors and villagers

Psychologists have discovered a fundamental difference in how the majority of men and women in our culture are shaped at the deepest reaches of our beings. For a variety of reasons, whether conscious or unconscious, most men experience life as a contest, battle or struggle. Most of the people around them are experienced as opponents, adversaries—even enemies. "Winning" or "losing" always hangs in the balance. Life is, in essence, combat—to be approached as a "warrior" would.

John is a department head whose favorite expression is, "Life's a football game." He guards his "turf" obsessively, supervises his staff with military efficiency, views other managers as rivals and assumes that other managers see him the same way. John is tough, but fair. And he is known as someone who plays "hardball." John is a warrior.

Most women, by contrast, live in a less threatening world. Experts claim that, consciously and/or unconsciously, the majority of women are driven more to form relationships with other people than to defeat them. These women see other people as partners and friends, not foes. And they seek intimacy with them. Most women experience life in a way that is analogous to living in a town or village where the lives and interests of all of its members are intimately connected. For most women, then, life isn't a contest, but a community—to be approached as a "villager" would.

Nancy is a manager who makes it a point to start every Monday by asking each member of her staff, "How was your weekend?" She believes that this helps people ease back into the job and get to work faster. Then at 10 a.m. she calls a meeting. She makes it clear what she wants done for the week, but she leaves it up to her subordinates to decide how to do it. Nancy is a villager.

It's hard to imagine a more dramatic difference than between approaching life as a warrior and approaching life as a member of a close-knit community. It's easy to understand, then, why experts claim that men and women live in different worlds. For most men, walking out the door in the morning is tantamount to heading for some kind of battlefield where their adversaries await them. For most women, by contrast, it's like going to the town square where they'll find friends, neighbors and relatives.

Which are you?

Now take a look at the score from your questionnaire. Obviously, if your "W" score is higher than your "V" score, you're a "warrior." If it's the other way around, you're a "villager."

What does your score really reveal?

Primarily, it shows how you experience life at a deep psychological level and how your behavior reflects that fact. (And don't be surprised if you're a male villager or female warrior. Remember, the connection between gender and personality differences isn't rigid.) But what does it really mean to be a warrior or villager? Let's look at the differences in more detail.

Warriors

As we've mentioned, if you're a warrior, you actually experience life mainly as a contest with other people.

The world, for you, is a battlefield. Accordingly, you tend to be aggressive and competitive in your dealings with others. You're probably somewhat distrustful of them, assuming that they, like you, are out to "win." So in your dealings with other warriors, you try to be strategic, on guard and "on your toes." You probably resist asking other warriors for help because this will reveal some weakness of yours to them, and you may end up owing them something in return.

You're sensitive to what it takes in order to get ahead of others, to promote your own interests, and to intimidate other warriors. Accordingly, in order to let other warriors know that you're someone to contend with, you're comfortable "sparring" with them—in everything from being the center of attention in a group, to telling jokes, to matching one another in friendly insults or putdowns. You're probably highly motivated to be successful, and you may enjoy anything that shows how well you're winning in the game of life—money, promotions, expensive objects or the like.

You're especially sensitive to what is your "turf," and you aggressively defend what is yours. You know that for every winner there is a loser, and you consider compassion for your adversaries a weakness. The only warriors worthy of your respect are those who fight for what they believe. But the battlefield is a tough place, and knowing how to be clever and shrewd is as important as knowing how to use a sword.

As a warrior, you're unlikely to publicize your fears and weaknesses. Tending to your own feelings and those of the people around you is less important than strategizing about your current struggle. You're probably fairly good at being tough with people and looking after yourself. And all of this makes you less likely to invest your primary energies in intimate, emotional relationships.

This is not to say that you don't have friends. But you probably have only a small number of close friends, and they're more likely to be other warriors, not villagers. Warrior friendships are less personally revealing and emotionally intense than villager friendships. After all, it's difficult to shift gears from eyeing other people as adversaries to trusting them enough to put down your weapons and reveal your deepest feelings. You may very well find villager friendships draining and requiring too much effort. As a warrior, you can enjoy being with a friend even when no words pass between you. You're probably at your most relaxed when you talk with another warrior about the day's "battle." You and your warrior friends also probably share a keen interest in other "battles" around you, such as the competition involved in sports or politics.

You're a warrior, however, not a "barbarian." Warriors have codes and a sense of honor and fairness, even if villagers can't see this. It's true that the "rules of the game" may allow cunning, bluffing, plotting against other warriors and other things that villagers disapprove of. Nonetheless, warriors are ordinarily willing to stand or fall without complaint according to these rules, as long as they apply to everyone equally.

As a warrior, your primary strengths are self-confidence, going the distance in a struggle and getting what you want in life. You enjoy the role of protector and provider. As a warrior, you're probably a "take-charge" kind of person. When a situation needs a leader, you're ready to fill the bill. You're comfortable telling people what to do. And while you don't enjoy disciplining or firing people under you, you don't shirk from it when it's necessary. Your confidence serves you well in trying to convince other people of your point of view or in trying to sell something.

Another strength is that as a warrior, you generally like to be straightforward in your dealings with others. That is, you're a "no nonsense," "what you see is what you get" individual. Other people usually have no trouble knowing where they stand with you. If you're upset with someone about something, you'll let it be known, argue it out and put the issue behind you. You also try to be fair. Accordingly, in making decisions, you prefer to rely on objective measures that everyone can see and understand—things like numbers, rules, policies. As a result of all of these strengths, when other people disagree with you or even if they dislike you, they nonetheless respect you.

Being a warrior has its occupational hazards, however. You probably trust other people less than they deserve, and you may doubt the sincerity of genuinely altruistic people. You may see plots and conspiracies where none exist. Your drive to win may get you in trouble on occasion. You probably have some difficulty working very closely with other people—particularly if you see them as competitors—and you may alienate them in the process. Also, you're probably so good at projecting an image of confidence and competence that you might get jobs, assignments or promotions that you can't really handle. You most likely have trouble opening up and getting close to people. So you have more than your share of problems in personal relationships.

Villagers

If you're a villager, on the other hand, you experience life primarily as the member of a small, close-knit community. The world, for you, is a village. The most basic fact of your psychological life is that you see yourself as connected in a positive way to other people. Your primary motivations lie in developing strong relationships with the people around you. In essence, you're an expert in this area. You know how to put other people at ease. You probably open up to them about your hopes, fears and personal matters

quickly and easily, and they do the same in return. Your friendships are close and emotionally intimate, and they are probably one of the most valuable aspects of your life. Your relationships are harmonious. You consider "hidden agendas" and manipulation to be serious betrayals of trust.

You tend to be cooperative, even acquiescent, in your dealings with other people. One reason for this is that you very much want to be liked by the people around you. This makes you sensitive to their desires and to the dynamics of your relationships with people.

Another reason you're so cooperative is that you see the interests of everyone in the village as intertwined. If things are going well for you as the village cobbler, but going badly for the farmers, you're concerned. You know that their bad luck will eventually come to haunt you. You're usually willing to put your interest second to that of the group because, as you see it, either everyone in the village will succeed together or everyone will fail together. As a result, you're willing to ask other villagers for help and to help them without a sense that they are in your debt. You tend to trust other people and to assume that they are as concerned about the welfare of the group as you are.

An important part of what you see as necessary for the village's success is for everyone to get along. Thus, you'll probably do almost anything to avoid conflict. You're willing to shoulder more than your share of blame over a misunderstanding with someone for the sake of keeping peace. In order to let someone save face, you readily apologize or admit that you are wrong—even if you weren't really at fault. You want to be seen as friendly, cooperative, open and accessible—not intimidating. You tend not to interrupt other people when they talk. And you're so considerate of other people that, in a hallway or on a sidewalk, you'll usually move out of their way or walk around them.

You like to blend into a group, and you're uncomfortable with anything that makes you feel different from or separated from other people. Particularly on the job, you don't enjoy drawing attention to yourself or engaging in self-promotion. You probably say little at meetings, and you're certainly never the first person to speak. When someone praises or congratulates you, you probably "talk down" the compliment or minimize your accomplishments. You have such a strong concern for protecting other people's feelings and such an aversion to head-on competition that succeeding at someone else's expense takes some of the joy out of winning. Professional success is probably a two-edged sword for you. You enjoy the rewards of doing a job well, but you're uncomfortable with feelings of superiority over others.

As a villager, your main strengths lie in how you deal with other people.

You are sensitive, and your concern with others is genuine. This makes you an ideal person to work in a group or on a team. You're willing to work behind the scenes or to do unglamorous and unrecognized tasks that are nonetheless critical to the team's success. As a manager, you're willing to be flexible in dealing with your subordinates, and to make exceptions to rules or policies. As a leader, you're gentle and inclusive, making sure that everyone with a stake in some decision gets heard. You're also generous with praise and with sharing the credit for successes with other people. You're willing to listen to people's problems, something that helps stave off future difficulties. Your strengths also include a willingness to compromise and the ability to arbitrate disputes.

Of course, like warriors, villagers also have weaknesses. Your unaggressive nature means that you probably look after your own interests less effectively than warriors look after theirs. Wanting to be liked so much may lead you to be affected too much by what other people want, or by what they think of you. You probably trust other people too much. As a result, every now and then you get taken advantage of by people—and you're always surprised when it happens. You will remember who hurt you, however, because that person now registers as someone who is untrustworthy in your life. And you may hold onto hurts or bear grudges for a long time.

You blur your personal and professional relationships more than you should. And you can be overly emotional in professional relationships, taking offense where none was intended. Your discomfort with open conflict carries major drawbacks. You may not be completely honest with people, concealing things that you fear will upset them. As a result, you may have an unintentional tendency to be manipulative. And your anger and aggression towards others may come out behind their backs.

We've all got parts of both

The first thing that your questionnaire shows, then, is which of these two descriptions captures the main lines of your personality. In the end, we're all either warriors or villagers. We live in the middle of either a contest or a community.

Recall, however, that you came up with two scores—a "warrior" score and a "villager" score. (Very few people score 21 warrior or 21 villager.) This shows that all of us actually have both warrior and villager sides inside of us—even if one side is stronger.

Accordingly, your questionnaire shows just how pronounced this psychology is in you. That is, we differ from each other not only as warriors or villagers, but also in how strong those traits are in us. If your score was 11/10, both tendencies are fairly evenly matched in you. The closer you get to 21/0, however, the more pronounced is your disposition as a warrior or villager. Accordingly, we aren't talking about which of two boxes all of us fall into, but where we end up along a warrior-villager continuum.

Realizing that we're talking about a continuum should explain some things about yourself and about other people. Those individuals in the middle of the continuum can probably shift between warrior and villager modes fairly easily, but this would be much more difficult for people at the ends of the spectrum. This could explain why some people are more flexible than others in certain situations. It could also explain why some people are so firmly committed to certain principles that they'll stick to them even when it's to their disadvantage to do so.

Roger is a consummate warrior with such an unshakable commitment to honesty that he refuses to tell "white" lies, even if it means hurting someone's feelings and appearing insensitive.

Grace is an extreme villager who puts such a premium on loyalty that she sticks by people who take advantage of her.

Realizing that all of us have both warrior and villager tendencies also should make it easier for you to understand people of the opposite type. If, as a villager, you're aware that you have a warrior side of your own, you can understand warriors more easily and more sympathetically than if you believed that you and they were cut from completely different kinds of cloth. Before you use "barbaric warrior" or "weak villager" as an epithet to criticize someone's behavior, examine the flip side of your own coin. Look at the times when you act opposite to your main tendencies, and try to sympathize with what might be motivating that person.

Your "other side"

Realizing that you have an opposite side, even if weaker, can also help you cope with difficult situations. If you're a warrior dealing with villagers, try to access the side of you that's comfortable letting down your guard and making people feel at ease with you. If you're a villager competing against warriors, get in touch with the thrill of victory and the pleasure associated with projecting an image of strength.

Your flip side might actually automatically surface at different times. So be alert to times when you, normally a warrior, start acting like a villager, and vice versa. And don't be surprised when other people "flip" as well.

Identifying the natives

Now that you have a basic grasp of the distinguishing traits of warriors and villagers and see which you are, think about different people in your life and come up with two lists. Who are the warriors? Who are the villagers? Who are the extreme examples of each? And who fall more into the middle of the range?

The first thing you should notice is that, more often than not, your list of warriors will mainly be men, and your villagers will mainly be women.

The second thing you should notice, however, is that each of your two lists should actually have both men and women on them. Although in the majority of cases, warriors and villagers fall along gender lines, a sizable minority of people cross over from what you'd expect from gender alone. You won't have to look far to discover female warriors and male villagers. Many women are warriors by nature. Many have become warriors as a way of competing with men in the workplace. A surprising number of men are villagers. In fact, in our work, we've come across more male villagers than female warriors. So when you try to figure out whether someone's a warrior or villager, don't get fooled by their sex. Focus instead on their basic personality traits.

And just in case you're having trouble figuring out who's who, at the end of this chapter is a lighthearted list of hints.

Why are warriors "warriors" and villagers "villagers"?

As a result of understanding the personality differences we've been discussing, you should now be able to determine whether you're a warrior or a villager. You should also be able to figure this out about the people around you at work.

You might be curious to know why we turn out as we do. What makes some of us warriors and others villagers? If gender is not the reason, what is?

For those of you who enjoy theoretical explanations, you'll find a full answer to this question in Chapter 6. So if you like theory, go read that now before you read Chapter 2. However, if you just want to know enough to help you with the practical side of life, here are the main reasons. This will be good enough for now, and you can read the full story later.

It's all about safety and danger

Ultimately, what we're talking about with warriors and villagers are differences at a deep psychological level in what makes people feel safe or in danger. What determines whether we're warriors or villagers is what, at the core of our being, makes us feel secure or threatened. The most fundamental and most powerful psychological difference between warriors and villagers is that, in the deepest reaches of their souls, warriors and villagers have opposite ideas about what counts as safety and what counts as danger.

What are these differences? And how do they determine whether we're warriors or villagers?

The simplest way of putting this is as follows.

1. A critical psychological fact about all of us is how we picture ourselves. When the world lets us live in a way that agrees with this picture of who we are, we feel safe and secure. But if the world makes it difficult for us to live according to this picture, we actually feel, at an unconscious level, that we're in danger.

2. In the deepest reaches of their psyches, warriors picture themselves as solitary and independent individuals; the greatest threat to this autonomy is being under the control of others. Villagers, by contrast, see themselves as being essentially connected to other people; separation from others feels dangerous.

3. Thus, no matter what it looks like on the surface, warriors act as they do in order to protect themselves from other people taking away their independence. Villagers act as they do in order to avoid being alone in the world and having no one to rely on.

4. In other words, we're warriors or villagers because of what it takes for us to feel safe in the core of our souls.

Other people, safety and danger

In terms of the psychology involved, the critical fact that defines warriors and villagers is how they regard other people. Living as they do in the middle of a battlefield, warriors see other people primarily as adversaries, that is, sources of danger. Living in a close community, villagers see the people around them as friends and neighbors, that is, sources of safety. Warriors do know that some other warriors can be allies, and villagers are aware that some villagers are untrustworthy, but their automatic reactions to other people are distrust and trust, respectively.

In their ordinary dealings with other people, then, warriors (mainly men) try to enhance their own power or status in order to decrease their unconscious fear of being dominated or hurt by others. Similarly, villagers (mainly women) try to develop equal and cooperative relationships in order to decrease the unconscious fear of being abandoned by others. It may not look like this on the surface. A warrior may seem arrogant and self-serving. A villager may appear weak and obsequious. In reality, they're both driven by opposite (and unconscious) ideas of how threatening other people are. And they're both just trying to feel safe.

Keep this basic difference between warriors and villagers in mind as you observe them in business. We guarantee that if you do, you'll have an easier time figuring out how to deal effectively with someone very different from yourself.

Warrior and villager fun facts

Warriors

In a warrior's office, you'll find a football, baseball, basketball, basketball hoop, dart board or target made from someone's picture.

Warriors study karate.

Warriors fantasize about swimming with sharks.

When warriors meet, they "rib" or jokingly "insult" one another.

Warriors like to use military, hunting or sports terminology when talking about almost anything.

When warriors go shopping, they go on a "hunt." Warriors shop alone. If they fail to "bag" something, it was a failure.

Famous warriors

Vince Lombardi
Murphy Brown
Norman Schwarzkopf
Margaret Thatcher
Joan of Arc
Gordon Gekko (from "Wall Street)
Lt. Worf
Lucy (from "Peanuts")
Kwai Chang Caine (from "Kung Fu)
The great white shark from Jaws
Madonna

Villagers

In a villager's office, you'll find a calendar from the Sierra Club or Greenpeace.

Villagers study tai-chi.

Villagers fantasize about swimming with dolphins.

When villagers meet, they hug.

When villagers speak, they try to be "politically correct."

When villagers shop, it's a social event. They go with other villagers. There's no such thing as a failed shopping trip.

Famous villagers

Joyce Brothers
Mr. Rogers
Bill Cosby
Eleanor Roosevelt
Ghandi
Ben and Jerry
Lt. Columbo
Charlie Brown
Kwai Chang Caine (some *are* both)
Barney the Dinosaur
Michael Bolton

Warrior and villager fun facts

Favorite warrior business books

The Leadership Secrets of Attila the Hun

Games Mother Never Taught You

Favorite warrior movies

"The Magnificent Seven"

"Rocky"

"The Terminator"

What you'll find in a warrior's pockets

Swiss army knife

High blood pressure medicine

Favorite warrior expression

"Winning isn't everything, it's the only thing."

Favorite villager business books

Getting to Yes

Anything by Tom Peters

Favorite villager movies

"Casablanca"

"Sleepless in Seattle"

"Rain Man"

What you'll find in a villager's pockets

Address book

Aspirin (for other people)

Favorite villager expression

"Make love, not war."

Chapter Two

Warriors and villagers at work

Handling a dispute between two of her people was the last thing Marilyn wanted to do before leaving for her vacation. But the situation between George and Megan had become too serious to ignore. What had been an usually good professional relationship between the two had deteriorated precipitously as a result of the incident. Normally, Marilyn wouldn't ask both parties to come in together. George, after all, was Megan's boss. But Marilyn was George's boss, and Megan had complained to her about the situation. Marilyn knew them both well, thought highly of each of them, and was puzzled about the problem. Marilyn had checked with the two of them, and both agreed to the joint meeting. Besides, there was no secret about what had happened. Marilyn was sure that there was no one on the seventh floor who didn't already know what happened and how George and Megan had reacted.

"I've called both of you in here," began Marilyn, "to see if we can straighten things out between the two of you. I'm not happy that things have blown up like this. But let's see if we can do some damage control. George, if you don't mind, I'd like to hear Megan's version of this first."

"I don't think there's any debate about the basic facts," explained Megan. "As part of my bid for a promotion, I was interviewed by George. In the course of the interview, George asked me to describe my weaknesses. I candidly listed the areas that I thought needed strengthening, and I described how I was working to improve them. A week later, George told me that the promotion was going to Ray. I asked why I'd been passed over, and in the course of his explanation, George focused on the very things that I had cited as my weaknesses. I was stunned and felt betrayed. I never imagined that George would use my own words against me like this."

"Do you have anything to add, George?" queried Marilyn.

"Not really," he said. "As Megan said, there's no argument between us about the facts. Of course, as I think everybody in the building knows by now, when I told Megan about my decision to give the job to Ray, she accused me of setting her up. And she didn't tell just *me* that. She told anyone who'd listen. I'm really offended that she thinks I deliberately tricked her, and I'm angry that she's going around telling this to other people. What reason would I have for creating a charade just so that I could promote Ray? I had plenty of good reasons for believing he was the best candidate. And, yes, the difference in how Ray and Megan handled my question about their weaknesses was one of them.

"But more important than that was that I felt that Ray would simply fit into the management team better. I can't completely put my finger on it, but I just feel more comfortable around Ray than I do around Megan. And as subjective as that might be, I think this is an important factor. After all, how well the work gets done around here depends a lot on how well people get along together.

"Frankly, I feel that Megan is being childish and spiteful and that she's trying to get even with me for not getting what she wanted. I'm amazed that she'd act so unprofessionally."

"Megan?" asked Marilyn.

"Well, what George said is true," conceded Megan. "But how could he expect me to think that he hadn't duped me? I trusted George with what I considered to be confidential information about myself. I can't believe that George acted so unprofessionally as to use that information against me. Maybe I shouldn't have talked to so many people, but they're entitled to know what kind of a boss they have. If George is this untrustworthy, I didn't want the same thing to happen to anyone else in the division.

"And while it's true that 'fitting in' and feeling comfortable with one another are important, why is it that when people in this company make decisions about promotions, it seems to be men who 'fit in' best most often? In all honesty, Marilyn, I've already started looking elsewhere. Some damage you can't repair."

....

What happened? What was the source of the misunderstanding between Megan and George? And, more importantly, what could each have done to avoid this problem?

The story of Megan and George is a perfect example of the problems that can arise between warriors and villagers on the job as a result of their not being sensitive to the considerable differences between them. Let's assume that both individuals acted in this situation in good faith. However, their conflicting assumptions about what was going on led to disaster, and an otherwise positive relationship was irrevocably damaged. It could also cost the company money in lost efficiency, lost productivity and, in the likely event that Megan leaves, lost talent. Alas, this kind of misunderstanding happens all too frequently in the workplace.

Subsequent chapters will look at specific topics—teamwork, leadership, giving one another a hard time and sexual harassment. In this chapter we'll give you an overview of how the personalities and world views of warriors and villagers produce some fundamental differences in how warriors and villagers approach the workplace. We'll see how each has very different ideas about what the point of work is, what counts as success, and what amounts to appropriate and inappropriate behavior in the pursuit of success. And we'll look at what Megan and George could have done to avoid their difficulties.

The workplace: the battlefield versus town square

We discussed in the last chapter that the fundamental psychological differences between people divide us into two categories—warriors and villagers. Since this amounts to basic differences in personality type, the way that life is experienced, unconscious feelings of safety and danger, and what feels most comfortable in dealing with other people, it should come as no surprise that warriors and villagers also have very different attitudes about work and the

workplace. In fact, warriors and villagers will even generally give you different explanations about what "business" is.

The most basic point to see is that when warriors and villagers walk through the same entrance to their jobs, they actually enter two totally different—*and unrelated*—places! Warriors go through the door and find themselves on a *battlefield*. Villagers walk through the same door and step into some community's *village square*.

For warriors, work is about looking for victory. Warriors and their corporate comrades struggle as a group against warriors from other businesses in the day's contest for customers, sales and profits. At the same time, however, warriors also compete against members of their own company for recognition, bonuses, promotions—that is, *individual* success, money and power.

For villagers, work is different. Villagers gather in the "square" to compare notes about what needs to be done in the village, to inventory which villagers have the needed resources and abilities to contribute, and to build a consensus about how to proceed. Work is about cooperating with other members of the company to advance the good of the group. However, in the same way that warriors have an individual agenda, villagers have a sense of community and positive connections with others.

Once again, we can't emphasize enough that neither way of approaching the workplace is better than the other. But they are profoundly different. And each outlook has its advantages and disadvantages.

Warriors on the job: the battlefield, the hunt, the army

Whether warriors consciously feel this way or not, when they arrive on the job every day, they step onto a battlefield. However, the workplace isn't some arbitrary battlefield where they fight simply for the sake of fighting. It's more serious than that. In fact, we might say that for warriors, work is in many ways the equivalent of the hunt for food. Succeeding on the job gives warriors the means of getting food, shelter, and clothing for themselves and for those under their care. How well warriors perform on "the hunt" determines whether they and their families will survive, and whether their lives will be ones of hardship or comfort.

Doing badly on the hunt is something of enormous consequence for warriors because it means that their lives are now literally at risk. A bad day for warriors on a hunt means that warriors don't eat tonight. But more than that, it means that they face tomorrow's hunt weakened and hungry. So warriors who have a bad day understandably get stressed and anxious.

Even good days on the hunt, however, let warriors relax only so much. Warriors still worry about whether they'll be successful tomorrow.

Thus, the world-picture that warriors have of life as a contest, a battle or a hunt contains the seeds of a deep sense of insecurity. In competing against other warriors for food in the hunt, warriors take nothing for granted. Warriors know too well that life has no guarantees and that complacency can be fatal.

The army

In light of these dangers and insecurities, warriors often band together and form *armies*. A military unit is orderly and efficient. So in this way warriors reduce their individual risks on the battlefield, and they increase their chances of success in the hunt. Despite the fact that warriors generally see themselves as strong and autonomous individuals, they seem to readily accept the logic of cooperating with one another in military units.

There are tradeoffs, however. Warriors must give up being independent, and they must now follow orders. And warriors are keenly aware that the best place to be is in charge. So warriors must now also compete against other warriors in trying to rise in the chain of command.

How warriors react on the job

A warrior's sense that going to work is like being in a battle against other warriors, going on a hunt, or being part of an army, then, makes the workplace a high-risk environment. Warriors are well aware of the insecurity of their situation. There are no guarantees in business. All warriors know respected colleagues who are now unemployed because of restructurings, downsizings, mergers or acquisitions.

Because warriors experience the workplace at a deep, psychological level, notice what follows:

1. The idea that warriors are part of an army explains the preference that corporate warriors have for a military model of authority in business. If a company's in a battle, this is the most sensible way to organize things. To look at the organizational chart of most businesses is to look at something resembling a military hierarchy. Positions have rank and authority. Higher positions generally grant power over a greater number of people (troops). Decisions handed down from above are seen as "orders" that subordinates must follow.

2. The idea that business is basically a contest explains *why so many warriors speak about business in military, hunting or sports terms*. For them, business literally is a battle.

- There are "sales campaigns" and "advertising campaigns." In the same vein, there's "market penetration" and "corporate strategy."

- In some companies, people inquire about where someone ranks in the hierarchy by asking, "Where is she in the food chain?"

- Faced with the prospect of cutting one's losses, it's not unusual for someone to suggest that "It's time to drop back and punt."

- One way of saying that a deal is guaranteed is: "It's a slam dunk."

- For some executives, a favorite way of saying that an apparently risky strategy is a "sure thing" is: "We're bulletproof on this one."

- Many business advice books pick up the battle or sports image: *The Warrior's Edge, The Genius of Sitting Bull, The Leadership Secrets of Attila the Hun.* Business advice books specifically for women also reflect this: *Hardball for Women*, and the classic *Games Mother Never Taught You* (with its chapter, "You're in the Army *Now*").

3. The attitudes that are appropriate to a battle or hunt explain why for warriors, a critical part of succeeding in business is to manage other people. Given the warrior's "contest" psychology, his best bet for safety is to be in command. The more one is a foot soldier, the more one is at risk. The best spot is to be in charge (and, if it's necessary, to be able to get a share of what other warriors catch on the hunt). The more people that corporate warriors have under them and the larger the budgets

they have command over, the greater their resources to muster against competitors. That's why, for warriors, success in business isn't being the best accountant, but being in charge of all the accountants. Warriors seem to have a powerful desire to be leaders.

4. Seeing business as a contest also accounts for the fact that, for many warriors, *dollars are "points."* Of course, all of us need money in order to pay for what we need, and we're motivated to make more money in order to be more comfortable or secure. However, warriors also see money as an indicator of how well they're winning. This makes the workplace like a sports contest. That is, it's a battle where winning and losing are determined by points, rather than body count. This explains a number of things.

- The fact that some warriors are always looking for a financial reward for their successes. (It's an empty exercise where there are no "points" associated with scoring.)

- The great concern of some warriors with how their salaries and bonuses stack up against those of other warriors. (It's not that they're being petty and greedy. They just want to outscore the competition.)

- The fact that warriors generally have few complaints about the large (sometimes huge) compensation packages that senior managers receive. (It makes as little sense to say that someone is "overpaid" as it is to say that one team scored "too many points" against another.)

5. If business is a battle or hunt, it is then logical that a warrior on the job would never be satisfied! That is, it makes sense that nothing in business would ever be enough. And this explains a number of characteristic traits of many warriors.

- The idea that "you're only as good as your next sale," and a warrior boss's question, "So what did you do for me *today?*" (As on the hunt, yesterday's successes are meaningless in the face of today's needs.)

- An obsession with increasing a company's profits, even in flush years; a never-ending drive to outperform last quarter or last year—even if the company enjoyed record profits. (The more money and power a corporation has, the more security it has in the present and the more flexibility it has for the future.)

- Trying to absolutely dominate a market—even if it means squeezing out small, apparently harmless competitors. (A company is secure only when there are no other competitors.

As we know from Apple Computers, operations that start in someone's garage can become financial giants.)

- A preoccupation with increasing one's personal fortune. (Nothing less than a huge amount of money can genuinely ensure financial security.)

- Insatiable ambition. (The only time a warrior is ever really safe is when he or she is totally in charge.)

6. This battle or hunt psychology even makes the fixation of some corporate warriors with the short run in business seem sensible. (If you fail in this week's contests, you may not be around for next week's.)

7. Experiencing business as a battle and a hunt has major implications for what warriors just naturally assume are *the traits needed to succeed in business*. Warriors think that you need to be like them—aggressive, strategic, strong, confident and savvy. Warriors may, then, have an automatic tendency to misunderstand villagers and to misread their strengths as weaknesses. In particular, warriors have a tendency to mistake a villager's cooperativeness for weakness, and a villager's being quiet as stemming from a lack of intelligence. (As we'll see at the end of this chapter, this is one of the factors that contributed to the difficulties between Megan and George.)

Things aren't necessarily what they seem

We want to take pains to point out that as in the case of the feelings about safety and danger that we pointed to at the end of the last chapter, and as we explain more in Chapter 6, the sense of being in a battle or "on the hunt" may be outside a warrior's conscious awareness. Therefore, a warrior's actions on the job may suggest something very different from what things look like. It may look like a warrior is driven by ego, greed or a need to win. It may even feel that way to the warrior himself or herself. Yet in reality, the warrior is driven by a deep worry that is absolutely logical, reasonable and prudent given a warrior's world-picture.

Warrior strengths and weaknesses

The outlook and attitudes we've been talking about are all sensible as long as the warrior's assumption that "business is war" holds. And, obviously, to a considerable extent, this is an apt metaphor. The free market is nothing if not competitive, and there are no guarantees. With the noteworthy exceptions of government "bailouts" of corporations like Chrysler and Lockheed, there is nothing to protect a company from going out of business. The vagaries of the marketplace are inevitable and unpredictable. And no one is immune. Even giants like IBM have felt the shock of a shifting economy. The same story holds for individuals. There's never a shortage of capable people vying for good jobs. And talent and experience aren't enough to protect everyone's job from the ebbs and flows of business—takeovers, bad timing, restructuring, bad luck.

In view of these characteristics of business, a warrior's approach offers many strengths. Refusing to be complacent, always looking for new opportunities, relentlessly searching for better ways of doing things, aggressively working for the company's interest, self-promotion, being obsessed with high-quality results, and enthusiastically embracing a spirit of head-on competition—all of these can contribute powerfully to individual and corporate success. When a problem has been talked to death, when it's time for action, when it's imperative to keep a sharp eye on the bottom line, and when deadlines are critical, a warrior's single-mindedness, decisiveness and desire for action are godsends. Particularly in difficult times, a warrior's willingness to look at the "big picture" objectively and to make hard choices can spell the difference between success and failure.

However, there's a catch to all of this. As much as business may in some ways be like a battle or like a hunt, we can't forget that business is, after all, simply business. That is, as competitive or war-like as business may get, business is primarily about a group of people making goods or offering services and trying to sell them to other people. Customers aren't adversaries

or prey. They're people with whom your business wants a long, supportive and mutually satisfying relationship. Competitors are simply that—competitors—not enemies. And for all of the military rhetoric that might be used, the major force that "defeats" any company isn't its competitors, but customers who decide to take their dollars elsewhere.

And from this vantage point, the idea that business should be viewed as a battle may push some warriors down a questionable path. Some warriors may pay less attention than they should to how well the people they work with or who work for them are getting along. (This, doubtless, feels like a luxury in the trenches.) Like the stock market, some warriors may overreact. News that, while not good, is only marginally bad may feel much worse to warriors than it actually is. When times are tight, some warriors might panic and overestimate how much money can be saved by letting some people go.

A fixation on the dynamics of conflict could make some warriors too concerned with the short-term in business. (They may focus on "battles" instead of "wars.") They may blindly accept decisions made by a superior when it's actually in the best interest of the company to challenge them. And their decisive nature may lead warriors to act impulsively when patience is more appropriate. Companies generally don't stand or fall on one deal. It's sometimes cheaper in the long run to

ride out entire downturns without firing anyone. And in order to achieve
maximum success, it is critical to tend
to the intangible dimensions of the
business—the relationships between
people.

Unfortunately, every now and then
you'll meet warriors who are so extreme
in their outlook that it impedes their
ability to approach a problem in a businesslike fashion.

*Mac is an "over-the-top" warrior
for whom business is, in reality, more
about ego and being in charge than
about making money. When Quan Li,
an investor in Mac's business, aggressively suggested that he pursue a seg-
ment of the market that Mac's competitors were overlooking, Mac felt so
challenged that he arrogantly insulted
Quan Li and her business savvy, and he
flatly refused to consider the new strategy. Now doubting Mac's abilities,
Quan Li pulled her money out of Mac's
business. Mac remains convinced that
he's right, even though an objective
analysis of the situation would reveal
that he passed up a major opportunity.*

Sadly, when you meet such a warrior in business, you have few options
because you're never going to win. Cut
your losses and move on.

For warriors, then, the workplace is
a place of risk and conflict. To the
extent that business is in fact a highly
competitive proposition, then, warriors

bring great strengths to the task.
However, to the extent that business
depends on harmonious and cooperative relationships among people, warriors may be at a disadvantage.

Villagers: the square, the meeting, the marketplace

Villagers walk through the same
entrance that warriors do at the start of
the workday, but they arrive someplace
different. Warriors stride into the middle of a contest, while villagers feel
like they're walking into the center of
the community—the "village square."

But don't be fooled by the fact that
the "square" is a more peaceful place
than the "battlefield" or the "hunt." The
situation may be less dramatic for villagers, but it's no less serious. After all,
the square is where villagers gather in
order to conduct the business of the village and to get what they need. This is
where the decisions are made that
affect them all. This is where they get
food, clothing, and whatever else they
need to survive.

The village meeting: democracy

To say that the workplace is like the
square where villagers handle the affairs
of the village, however, is to reveal one
of the most important differences
between warriors and villagers—their
attitudes about authority and about
telling people what to do.

In the village square, decisions
flow from a "meeting." Unlike armies,

villages are democratic. But don't think that a village's democracy is a luxury. That is, villagers aren't simply indulging themselves in coming to decisions jointly because they aren't in the middle of a battle. The main reason villages are democratic is that villagers are convinced that this is the most efficient and most effective way of ensuring the village's welfare. Villagers believe that if all villagers participate in the discussion about the state of the village, this will reveal the most complete picture of the village's needs and resources. Villagers also think that letting everyone have a say during the meeting makes it more likely that everyone will actually do his or her part in carrying out joint decisions.

A right to know

It should be apparent that the military idea that people are entitled to certain information only when they have a *need* to know makes absolutely no sense to a villager. Warriors may think that it's a virtue to follow orders. But villagers feel that they're entitled to know about whatever bears on the interest of the village. It is a core conviction that if a decision will have an effect on a villager, he or she has a right to be involved in it. And villagers feel this way particularly strongly about actions that they are being asked to carry out.

Consensus

When villagers approach a problem in a village meeting, then, they always strive to reach a consensus. Villagers believe that the best decision is the one that everyone agrees on. And because of this, they will spend what seems like inordinate amounts of time listening to one another's viewpoints until they reach a mutually satisfactory decision.

Village relationships

Finally, villagers see the village meeting as an important way to learn about other villagers. Both the formal and informal comments that villagers make at meetings, and the way that they treat other villagers, reveal much about their character and personalities. This gives villagers a clearer sense of just who makes up the village. It lets them know who they want to know better and get closer to. And it also reveals who they will be somewhat cautious towards.

The village market

When villagers go to work and enter the village square, they also step into the village market. And this is another major difference between warriors and villagers. Warriors acquire food and clothing through the "hunt" and through battling other warriors. But villagers get these things through trading with one another in the village market.

It's important to see, however, that while villagers are engaging in business, their motive is not solely individual profit. The market is set up to promote the general welfare of the community. The "village market" is designed to foster the welfare of all villagers as much as the village meeting does. Indeed, villagers see the purpose of the market so much as advancing everyone's interest that they think that kindness and generosity should be as much a part of what goes on as good deals and fair exchanges. So if one villager falls on hard times, other villagers are expected to help. In fact, in the village, the idea that villagers should help one another in the market is so strong that it is a central tradition in the village. Villagers virtually take it for granted that if other villagers are made aware of their need for help, someone will respond. Compassionate villagers are expected to sell on credit, drop their prices, even charge the needy villager nothing for goods. After all, villagers know that bad luck will eventually make its way around to all of them.

How villagers react on the job

A villager's perception of the workplace is obviously very different from the warrior's. Entering the village square is much less risky than stepping onto a battlefield. But survival—of the individual and the group—is still what's at stake. Moreover, being a villager carries with it a stronger sense of being a member of a group, more responsibilities to others and a greater sense of self-sacrifice than being a warrior does.

To villagers, work is very different from how warriors see it.

- Work's primary purpose is less about winning than about

working together to do something useful.

- Villagers think that business operates best if people cooperate with, not compete against, one another. Even very ambitious villagers think that it's better for business to be conducted harmoniously. Villagers tend to view the people around them as allies to be empowered, not adversaries to be bested.

- Work is about being involved in doing something that the group believes is important.

Experiencing the workplace this way explains much about villagers' preoccupations on the job.

1. The fact that villagers experience the workplace as something akin to the village square explains why so many corporate villagers emphasize consensus-building, involving many people in any decision, getting people to "buy in" to any new program, and making sure that everyone understands the rationale behind any significant decision or policy.

2. In the same spirit, this explains why, as a rule, villagers behave differently at meetings than warriors do.

- Villagers tend to be relatively quiet at meetings, listening more than they speak.

- They press their own point of view less aggressively than warriors do.

- Villagers are generally more patient than warriors with meetings that aren't immediately productive. Villagers see benefit in allowing everyone who wants to speak an opportunity to be heard. Villagers believe that this increases positive, cooperative feelings among people involved in a process. Villagers also want to be sure that all of the information or viewpoints relevant to a decision get out on the table.

3. Seeing the workplace as the village square explains why villagers constantly stress the importance of tending to relationships—with customers, with vendors, with co-workers, with subordinates, with bosses. (It's self-defeating to alienate anyone in the village with whom you're going to have ongoing relationships.)

- Accordingly, villagers are not "policy people." To villagers, tending to relationships means being aware of the unique character of every relationship. And this means that villagers are generally willing to make exceptions to policies, and to adopt an *ad hoc* approach to problems.

- Villagers have a tendency to ask other people's permission too frequently before they do something. To warriors, this looks like a weakness and an inability to take initiative. But villagers are trying to preserve good relationships with those around them.

4. The "workplace as village" explains why so many villagers prefer more participatory forms of management. Villagers prefer "horizontal management," allowing decisions to be made at low levels of responsibility, and "empowering" subordinates.

5. Villagers usually arrange their office furniture so that there are no barriers—like desks—between themselves and other people. They're fond of having sitting areas in their offices. This preference also extends to the furniture arrangement in meeting rooms. Villagers prefer egalitarian arrangements: movable furniture, chairs in circles, tables without "power positions," and the like.

6. The village emphasis on cooperation, self-sacrifice, and advancing the interest of the group makes corporate villagers less inclined to promote themselves and to advertise their accomplishments.

7. The idea that the workplace is a village also explains why villagers are responsive to the claim that business has a "social responsibility" to various constituents that rivals its financial responsibility to its owners and creditors. Villagers are fond of the idea that a corporation has a duty to recognize the interests of its various stakeholders.

8. The village's tradition of being sensitive to the needs of others makes villagers see layoffs, plant closings, downsizings and moving operations offshore only as strategies of last resort.

9. If the workplace is the village square, corporate villagers see the qualities needed to succeed in business as villager traits more than warrior traits. Being cooperative, open, responsive to others' needs and putting the interest of the group ahead of your own are considered more "businesslike" than being competitive, aggressive and strategic. This, of course, leads villagers to misread warriors. In particular, villagers can mistake a warrior's competitive move as a personal assault. That is, villagers can take the competition personally.

Villager strengths and weaknesses

As is the case with warriors, a villager's approach to business has both positive and negative sides. Perhaps the most important strength is that villagers in the square are trading. They aren't conducting business as aggressively as warriors would, but they are doing business nonetheless!

Of course, another major strength that villagers bring to business is their strong orientation to the "relationship" side of business. Villagers never forget that all of the numbers—EPS, dividends, P&L, quarterly earnings, the "bottom line"—result from the actions of individual human beings joined in a common effort. For villagers, business is ultimately about people—employers, employees, managers, customers, suppliers, lenders, investors, and the like.

Other strengths include: villagers' abilities to work with other people on teams; their willingness to accept comments about the business from any source and from all levels in an organization; loyalty; having less of a personal agenda than warriors do; and being willing to communicate and share information with other people in the organization.

Nonetheless, in our modern, highly competitive economy, business sometimes is very much like the battle that warriors feel it to be. And to this extent, a villager's outlook contains major liabilities. Villagers may fail to recognize that there is, at least to some extent, an adversarial component in business relationships, that is, between companies and their customers, stockholders, employers and suppliers. Villagers also may be less savvy than warriors in how to manage their careers and promote their private interests.

Another major weakness villagers bring to business, however, is the "flip side" of the warrior weakness of unwarranted impatience—and that is, the villager's unwarranted complacency. Many villagers believe so strongly that people should help one another and that things will somehow work out for the best that they sometimes do not take seriously enough the hard, unpredictable side of business. Some villagers cut chronically weak workers too much slack. These managers hope to turn poor workers around, but fail to recognize that they're straining their good employees' sense of fairness. Many villagers resist firing people more than they should.

Villagers bring great insight into the "people" side of business. Yet even good companies fail. Some employees never will work out. And in hard times, layoffs or moving operations offshore may actually be the only way for a company to survive. Sometimes aggressiveness, competitiveness and strategic ingenuity is the only way to succeed both as a business and as an individual working in a business. And at those times, villagers might be at a disadvantage.

As we saw with warriors, you'll occasionally find a villager who is so extreme that the imperatives of doing business pale in significance to being a villager.

Sandy is so extreme a villager that she never really "gets it" when her supervisor takes her to task for not paying enough attention to her job. When Sandy goes to work, her top priority isn't her duties as much as things like keeping up with the office gossip about co-workers' personal lives, organizing birthday lunches for people in the office, and consoling colleagues who are going through hard times. Sandy has been fired before because her bosses think that she simply isn't serious enough about what's important. The truth is that she is—only what's important to her is vastly different from what's important to them. Sandy cannot understand why she keeps ending up with such heartless supervisors who expect her to do more than is possible during a workday.

Assessing others

As much as whether someone's a warrior or villager explains their different attitudes about business, it explains even more how they evaluate other workers. There are three fundamental facts of human nature to keep in mind as we discuss the differences in how warriors and villagers assess other people on the job.

1. We all think that our ideas, values and practices are generally the best ones.

2. When we find people agreeing with us or doing things as we do them, we usually conclude that it's because of their superior intelligence, judgment and ability.

3. Even when we aren't consciously aware of it, people who are fundamentally different from us make us uneasy. Warriors and villagers alike can feel threatened by the differences between them.

"Mirror mirror on the wall . . ."

In our hearts, most of us are very comfortable with how we do most things in life. We may never let other people know this. Because being self-satisfied is more than a trifle arrogant, most of us probably even have trouble admitting to ourselves that we feel this way.

Nonetheless, most people are pretty comfortable with the way they go through life. Most people see themselves as good drivers, for example. (It's the other people on the road who create problems.) Similarly, most people think that their political views are on target, no matter how extreme they are. (They can't understand how there can be so many wrongheaded people in the world.) And even when they think there's something odd about people of a different race, gender, sexual orientation or ethnic background, they never see themselves as prejudiced. They may think unkind things about other people, but they believe they have good reason to be annoyed with them.

We view the world and other people, then, through the lens of our own preferred values, customs and prejudices. It's so automatic that we don't even think about it. Most of us just assume that our line on things is the right one.

Kindred spirits

A second fact of human nature is that when we meet people who see the world as we do, we all take things one step too far in the conclusions we draw about these individuals. Because most of us believe that our way of living and

thinking is the correct way, when we meet kindred spirits, we feel that we've met other right-minded people. That is, we see these people as being not simply like us. We see them as being like us in being right.

Moreover, we all believe that such like-minded people are that way because of their superior abilities. These are people of innate good sense, exceptional judgment and high intelligence. The fact that they agree with us proves that. And, of course, we're just as sure that people who disagree with us do so because, as Steve Jobs is fond of saying, "They're bozos."

It seems to be human nature to make virtues out of all of our traits—strong or weak. And we then judge other people accordingly.

It's all about safety and danger

Third, the reason we believe that people who see things differently from us are somehow wrong or inadequate is that we are actually frightened of them. Warriors and villagers alike may feel threatened by the differences between one another.

As we pointed out at the end of the preceding chapter, and as will be explained in more detail in the final chapter, both warriors and villagers feel that the opposite type in some way poses a danger to them. Villagers threaten a warrior's need for autonomy, control and independence. Warriors threaten a villager's need for closeness and connection. And we are simply more comfortable with people who don't threaten us.

The "comfort criterion"

The significance of these three factors is, not surprisingly, that they lead us to surround ourselves with people we feel are just like us. And that means that when we evaluate other people at work (when we interview someone for a new job, when we conduct performance appraisals, when we set raises, when we choose who will get a promotion), we have an almost instinctive preference for people who act like us. We just automatically assume that people like us are more capable than people with styles opposite our own. So one of the most important criteria we use for employment decisions is how *comfortable* we feel with someone.

Working together

Now from one point of view, there doesn't seem to be anything wrong with making employment decisions according to a preference for individuals with traits similar to our own and with whom we're most comfortable. It's critical for people to be able to work well together in business, particularly in this age of "teamwork." And we have to allow for a certain amount of intangible "gut feel" to be involved in determining whether we think someone will fit into a situation and be able to work with the people who are already on the job.

Moreover, the "comfort criterion" has clearly been at work in business for years. Employers hire, managers retain and bosses promote the people they feel most comfortable with. In fact, the most important factor in determining whether someone gets hired or promoted is probably whether the people making the decision feel that the candidate is "one of us." And if a preference for people similar to us leads to smooth operations and high productivity, why not go with it?

Human error

The problem with the three "facts of human nature" that we just described and that produce employment decisions that favor people "just like us," however, is that they're all totally false.

- Human fallibility guarantees that no matter how certain we feel about something, we are often wrong.

- People who think or do things differently from us are usually just as smart or as capable.

- Warriors and villagers aren't the enemies we fear they are.

And this means that the employment decisions we make based on a preference for people "just like us" will often be unfair because we will frequently pass over deserving candidates.

Not preference, but bias

The problem with the old tradition of preferring people that we're most "comfortable" with because they're "just like us," then, is that, for all the efficiency and smooth operations that it has produced, a great deal of harm has also resulted. For example, this preference has been one of the main forces behind outright discrimination in the workplace. After all, we aren't talking about a simple preference for working with one kind of person. We're talking about an unfounded bias and irrational prejudice against people different from us. This bias may stem from a common, and even understandable, psychological phenomenon among most humans—a deep-seated fear of people different from ourselves. But this doesn't change the fact that this fear is as wrong-headed as it is widespread, and that it has led to great injustice.

Discrimination

The most obvious example of the harm we're talking about is, of course, the racial and sexual discrimination that our society has been trying to eradicate over the last three decades. This prejudice is represented by those whose hatred and paranoia of people different from themselves lead them to proudly trumpet their conviction that women and non-whites are genetically inferior breeds who don't belong on an equal footing with white men and can't "cut it" in business.

However, as our society gets past barring African-Americans from the executive suite and paying lower salaries to women who did the same job as men, a more pernicious form of discrimination is quietly insinuating itself into the workplace. People who supported civil rights legislation and affirmative action programs and who were genuinely outraged by self-proclaimed racists, chauvinists and sexual predators nonetheless unwittingly continue these bigots' work by using the "comfort criterion"—refusing to hire or promote people who just didn't "fit in" for one reason or another.

The motivation of these business people is virtually always a sincere attempt to select people who would make the business run better. The problem is, however, that the leadership in business has for years been almost exclusively white, male, heterosexual and politically conservative. And that means that some people managers simply don't "feel comfortable" with are largely African-American, Hispanic, Asian, female, gay and left-wing. The "comfort criterion" may not have had the intention of treating people in business differently on the basis of their race, sex, ethnic background or sexual orientation. But it does have this practical effect in the workplace.

There is a major exception to the idea that the "comfort criterion" is generally used by warriors and villagers in a good faith attempt to improve the way the business runs—and that's when we're uncomfortable with someone because they're too much like us. Warriors and villagers alike who are insecure may fear that someone with similar or superior abilities may threaten the role they play in the office or organization. For example, someone may not want to hire a candidate they fear may take over their role of "office nurturer" or "office wit." And this insecurity leads them to feel so uncomfortable as to reject the candidate for selfish reasons. But in such cases, most of us are well aware of the fact that we're doing this and that we're being unfair.

Hitting the glass ceiling

Accordingly, after millions of dollars of special programs and after decades of concerted attempts by major corporations to eradicate discrimination in their ranks, we still hear complaints by various groups that they aren't able to advance in business according to their talents and get a fair shake. In retail stores, aspiring saleswomen complain that they're steered away from the big-ticket appliance departments and end up selling shoes. In large corporations, women complain that they're more likely hired into "staff" departments, while their male counterparts land in "line" functions. African-Americans protest that while their careers at first appear to run along the same track as their white colleagues, nonwhite executives rarely climb past a certain point in the hierarchy and enter the inner sanctum.

In short, people who are "different" find their careers dead-ending as they hit the infamous glass ceiling. The people who rise past them are no more talented than they are. Those who advance are simply more like the people who make the decisions. While it may not be the result of conscious racism and sexism, because of the comfort criterion, it's no accident that the upper slice of corporate America remains white and male.

Birds do it, bees do it, warriors and villagers do it

Of course, it's old news that race and sex consciously and unconsciously come to play so much in employment decisions that the glass ceiling is a real phenomenon. However, the fact that our proclivity to hire people we're "comfortable" with stems from such powerful factors, means that the phenomenon is much more widespread than most of us want to admit. It should come as no surprise, then, that all of this also surfaces in the way that warriors and villagers deal with each other.

The unquestioned belief that our way of thinking and doing things is the best way infects warriors and villagers alike. And the fear of people different from ourselves is especially pronounced between warriors and villagers. Accordingly, when warriors and villagers make employment decisions about each other, they invariably use the comfort criterion. And that means that there is probably just as much irrational prejudice and unfair discrimination in the workplace based on, shall we say, "typeism" as there is on racism and sexism.

However, because this kind of bias is usually between people of the same races and sexes, and because it's generally cloaked in legitimate "business" defenses, it's harder to recognize it for what it actually is. Nonetheless, it's just as hurtful. It's just as wrong. And it's just as indefensible as racial and sexual prejudice.

It ain't easy

Anyone who has tried to ride herd on the way that issues stemming from race and sex insinuate themselves into and undermine their evaluations of people knows how difficult this is to identify and remove. For example, senior executives have to catch themselves from thinking that speech patterns of other ethnic groups indicates that they are less educated than their colleagues. Similarly, male managers have to check themselves from suspecting that women on their staffs lack confidence and aggressiveness because they end so many sentences with questions and because they may cry when they're upset or angry.

However, as hard as it is to catch bias stemming from such obvious factors as race or sex, prejudice against warriors and villagers is actually much harder to recognize. Warriors don't see themselves as operating out of any kind of bias when they decide not to promote a man who isn't "hungry" enough. Villagers would be shocked at being labeled prejudiced at giving a subordinate low marks because she was "too pushy" and "uncooperative" in how she works with other members of her department. It's unquestionably harder

to conceive of these actions as potentially unfair than it is to worry whether similar actions may stem from racial or sexual stereotypes. We haven't trained ourselves to think that there may be ethical issues involved in our reaction to one another as warriors or villagers.

Bias against warriors and villagers may actually be harder to recognize, admit and correct than bias based on race, sex or sexual orientation. But it's just as real.

Megan and George revisited

If the first chapter of this book shows you how warriors and villagers live in different worlds, this chapter aims to show how these different psychologies produce very different attitudes about the workplace. Although warriors and villagers go through the same door at the start of the day, they end up in different places—one on the battlefield and in a hunt, the other in the village square.

But let's return to our opening story about Megan and George and see if what we've been talking about can explain what happened between them.

What happened?

Let's start with the idea that both Megan and George acted in good faith. Let's assume that George didn't "set up" Megan, that he believes he treated her fairly and that, in the end, he genuinely believed that she was not the best candidate. Let's also concede that

Megan was deeply hurt by what George did, that she honestly cannot see a positive interpretation of George's behavior, and that she's not just being vindictive. Let's work with what we've seen in this chapter about the general differences between warriors and villagers at work, and see if this can explain what went on.

In the competition among warriors, one of the accepted "rules of the game" is: "Conceal your weaknesses. Everyone has shortcomings, but advertising them to other warriors is dangerous. Warriors must always project strength in order to be taken seriously by other warriors. Those who don't know how to conceal their weaknesses are less effective leaders than those who do." That's why every book of advice for job seekers says that when asked what your weaknesses are, never give a straight answer. These books recommend that you phrase your answer in a way that really has you still describing your strengths. For example, "I work too hard" or "I'm too demanding on myself."

When George asked Megan about her weaknesses, then, he initially wasn't interested so much in what they actually were as how she'd handle this question. He was looking to see if she could conceal her weaknesses. How good a warrior was she? Could she project strength, confidence and self-assurance even when asked about her failings? When Megan answered as she did, George concluded that she lacked the savvy that the job called for. That is,

George viewed how Megan answered the question as a sign of how she would behave on the job in the future. George may even have thought that if Megan felt compelled to admit these particular weaknesses to him, then she must be aware that they were serious enough to hinder her performance in the new position. From his perspective, she was saying to him that she knew that she really was not fully qualified for the position. Otherwise, she'd see these shortcomings as inconsequential, and she would have finessed the question in a way that didn't even bring them up.

The traditions among villagers on this score are very different. Because everyone's interests are intertwined, villagers expect openness and candor in this situation. Among villagers, there is no dishonor in having weaknesses. The dishonor is in refusing to see them yourself (villagers prize self-knowledge) or in concealing them from other villagers. Hiding them says that you are more concerned with advancing your own interest than that of the village. Being less than fully candid when asked about shortcomings or problems that could affect other villagers is to reveal yourself as a selfish and untrustworthy villager. Thus, among villagers, being honest about your weaknesses is taken as a sign of strength and is generally praised.

As a villager, then, Megan assumed that George was asking for an honest answer. That is, Megan saw George's question as related more to the present than, as George saw it, to the future. She knew that George had the responsibility for making a good selection. And, knowing that everyone has weaknesses, Megan assumed that George really did need to know as much as he could about every candidate. Being candid showed that Megan respected George's predicament, that she was a genuine team player, and that she was so confident in her ability to do the job that she could even discuss her shortcomings. Her honesty also showed that she had a high degree of self-knowledge and that she was working on areas that needed improvement—traits that Megan took to be signs of strength.

Moreover, Megan felt that she already had a good relationship with George and that she could trust him with whatever she revealed about herself. When George used this information against Megan, she felt that he had betrayed her trust. Her only interpretation of the event was that George wasn't acting in good faith in the first place and was just trying to find an excuse to deny her the promotion.

George is also explicit about using the comfort criterion in deciding between Megan and Ray. And, as he explains, George thinks that this is a valid factor in business. As we've seen in this chapter, however, George may unintentionally be concluding which candidate is simply more like him, not which is more competent.

What we find, then, is that both George and Megan acted according to their respective natures as warrior and villager. They also behaved in keeping with the customs about assessing strengths and weaknesses "on the battlefield" and "in the village square." The problem, however, is that these traditions are diametrically opposed. And the inability of George and Megan to recognize those differences and to find their way through them had serious consequences.

What could George and Megan have done differently?

In light of what we know about warriors and villagers, how might George and Megan have done things differently and avoided this disaster?

First, Megan could have been more sensitive to the fact that warriors like George see the process of bidding for a promotion as a test. George's job is to find the best person for the position. And, given the way warriors see business, this means that George automatically assumes that he is looking for the best warrior. With this in mind, Megan could have been been more alert to the drawbacks of answering the question about her weaknesses as she did.

But how could she have answered the question without feeling that she was simply adopting a warrior mask and pretending to be someone that she isn't? Particularly since she already had a decent relationship with George, Megan could have diplomatically let it be known that she felt put on the spot. She could say: "I'd be lying or stupid if I told you I had no faults, and you'd be crazy to believe me. So, here are my weaknesses..." This would suggest that she trusted and respected him enough to give him a straight answer.

Or she might make it plain that she felt that she was in a no-win situation: "Look, George, for the sake of trying to make a good impression, I could say, 'I work too hard' or 'My standards for my subordinates are too high.' But if I give you a straight answer and everyone else you're interviewing finesses the question, then I'm going to be at a real disadvantage. I'm willing to give you all the information you need to make a good decision, but I don't want to deal myself out of the promotion because of it. How do you suggest we proceed?" This would at least reveal to George that Megan had a decent strategic sense and could spot a problematic situation.

At the same time, George could have been more aware of the fact that Megan was entrusting him with sensitive information about herself. George should have kept in mind that villagers like Megan want to be responsive and helpful to others—perhaps too much so. And they act this way especially when they've established a trusting relationship with someone, as Megan had with George. If George wants to know whether Megan can be savvy in some situation on the job—for example, if Megan can be strategic and knows how to conceal confidential information—

he should ask a different question. He should ask Megan something that is more obviously related to how she would perform in the position he's considering her for.

Warriors like George need to keep in mind that when villagers like Megan think about the traits that count as professional strengths, they automatically think about villager strengths, not warrior strengths. Had George interpreted Megan's answer accordingly, he would have had a different, and more accurate picture of Megan. And this also would have made it easier for him to assess Megan's strengths and weaknesses without relying on a vague and subjective sense of simply how "comfortable" he felt with her.

However, even if George still thought that Megan was the wrong person for the job, keeping her villager nature in mind would have let him better understand how to give her the bad news without having the situation blow up, as it did. Relying on what was publicly known about Ray and Megan, George could have spelled out why he thought that Ray was the better candidate without violating Megan's sense of trust.

George could also have taken pains to express some sympathy for Megan's disappointment, to remind her of her contributions to the organization, to praise her for her ambition, and to offer some advice that would help her advance the next time a promotion was possible. This would have communicated to Megan that George was aware of what was important to her and that he supported her. She still would have felt disappointed. But she also would have felt recognized and appreciated. She would have experienced George as a trustworthy—not unpredictable and dangerous—member of her village. And she would not have felt compelled to go around warning her co-workers about George.

Warriors and villagers on the job

Whether we're warriors or villagers, then, colors the way we look at business and has a profound affect on the way we approach our jobs. Overall, warriors are comfortable with an adversarial, win-lose, competitive, almost military character of doing business. Villagers, by contrast, prefer a more cooperative, relationship-driven and participatory view of the enterprise. And all of us have an almost instinctive preference for people "like us," which puts us at risk of using the comfort criterion more than we should. Whether someone is a warrior or villager explains a great deal about how we do our jobs, how we evaluate other workers and how we relate to co-workers, clients, vendors, and the like. And like our views toward life in general, warriors' and villagers' viewpoints about business can be extraordinarily different. Neither one is wrong. Each has strengths and weaknesses. But these differences must be recognized and appreciated.

Chapter Three

Teamwork and leadership

Laura is ready to hit the ceiling. She just finished her third straight meeting with Paul today in which she felt that her "partner" knifed her in the back. As Paul walks out of the conference room, Laura confronts him.

"Tell me," she began angrily, "do you care only about yourself, or do you not mind being so obvious about being two-faced?"

"Hey, what's this all about?" asked Paul, stunned at her verbal assault. "Selfish? Two-faced? Come on. We're on the same team here."

"Sure, that's what I thought until you turned on me. And not once, but three times today!" replied Laura.

"Turned on you?" asked Paul. "What's gotten into you Laura? What are you talking about?"

"First," she said, "it was that stunt you pulled this morning when we reported about our recommendation for pricing that new product line. Because you said you were so busy at the outset of this project, I agreed to do the tedious work of researching the prices of our main competitors and projecting the first year's sales. In exchange, you were supposed to take my data, formulate the recommendations, and present our findings."

"Right," admitted her co-worker. "And that's exactly what I did."

"Except you presented everything as though it was all your work," she remarked with annoyance. "Sure, you said it was a 'team' conclusion, a 'team' effort, and a 'team' decision. But that's not the way you came across. You never once pointed out anything specific that I'd done. And yet I did most of the work. You saw what happened after the meeting. Sanchez ignored me. But he complimented you, and then he hinted that he might put you on that product development task force at corporate."

"Look, I was just lucky. I can't control how a boss sees things. But I didn't turn on you," explained Paul.

"No, you just manipulated me to do your work, and then you took the credit," Laura complained. "And I suppose you're going to tell me that you didn't intentionally dominate today's project meeting just because Harrington showed up to see how we were doing. I'm the team leader on that project. Things are going well. And yet as soon as some VP steps into the room, you try to take over."

"You may be the team leader," replied Paul, "but we're all going to look bad if we don't finish on time. And I don't agree that things are going well. Don't take this personally, Laura, but you're a weak leader. You don't give the group any direction. All we do is talk about different possibilities. And everything's always a group decision. We waste too much time, and all the while the clock is ticking. Sure, I got nervous when Harrington showed up. But the group needs a strong leader, somebody who's not afraid of taking control, making decisions, and telling people what to do. I was just trying to move things along."

"You think I'm a weak leader? I suppose it might look that way if your hero is Genghis Khan," Laura observed. "But I was named team leader because I always bring projects in on time. Sure, I let discussions go until everyone's had a say. And I want decisions made by consensus. How else are you going to get everyone on board? How else can we figure out who's best for which task? But frankly, all of that's irrelevant. The point here is that you didn't have the courtesy to talk to me about being unhappy with the way things were going. You just decided to bulldoze your way into the limelight. And I'm sure it looked to everyone else on the team the same way it did to me. You weren't doing this because you care about the team or the deadline. You just wanted to look good at our expense—like what you did just now."

"Just now?" remarked Paul, astonished. "Nothing happened just now except that Goldberg didn't like our idea."

"Right," snapped Laura. "Only you left me holding the bag, even though you and I agreed on the strategy we'd push for. I sketched out our main ideas. Goldberg made noises that she didn't like that angle. And when I turn to you for support, I hear, 'Gee, Ilene, I hadn't looked at it that way.' You couldn't back away from our recommendations fast enough. You untrustworthy, self-serving turncoat. I can't believe that you bailed out on me like that!"

"Untrustworthy? This had nothing to do with trust. You saw as well as I did that she was married to another approach. It was foolish to disagree with her. It's stupid to stay with a sinking ship. There was no reason for both of us to look bad. Besides, I would have expected you to do the same if you were in my shoes. This was business; I didn't do you in. You just had a bad day. And I'm not thrilled that you're trying to blame me for it."

....

If there's one thing that defines "business"—after the fact that it's about making money—it's that people work together. With few exceptions, business is a group activity. People work in groups to make things. Teams of salespeople staff retail stores of all sorts to sell products. Offices are comprised of teams of people working in one department after another—accounting, human resources, operations, and the like. In addition, there's always someone charged with overseeing the group's work and with finding ways to help the group achieve its goals—a leader or manager. Teams and bosses are unchangeable features of the landscape of business.

One of the key differences between warriors and villagers, however, is that they have different ideas about what "teams" and "leaders" are and how they should behave on the job. This chapter will describe those differences, show how they produce the kinds of problems we just heard about from Paul and Laura, and suggest how to avoid them.

Warriors and villagers: two kinds of "teams"

One of the most important ways that people work together in business is on teams. Sometimes they're called *task forces*, *project groups*, *committees* or the like. But *teams* is probably the most

popular label in business these days. Many companies are talking about the importance of *teamwork*, and shifting the way that work is organized to *teams*.

We hear so much in business about teams and teamwork that it probably seems foolish to ask what a *team* is. But, without knowing it, warriors and villagers have very different ideas about what a team is and what counts as acceptable behavior for teammates. And this difference is one of the things that Laura and Paul ran into.

To villagers, a team is just a bunch of people getting together to perform a task that advances the welfare of the group. Yet to warriors, being on a team means being involved in conflict—both with an opposing team and, villagers will be surprised to hear, even with their own teammates. We find warriors and villagers living in very different worlds, and these differences can produce major problems when warriors and villagers end up on the same team together in business.

Villagers: "We're all in this together"

What is a team of villagers like? It's pretty straightforward: a group of people working together on some project that will benefit the "village." But remember how important *relationships* with others are to villagers. Villagers want to feel close to one another. They value harmony, and they want everyone to feel involved in group decisions. They'll make sure that everyone feels like they're part of the group, comfortable with the way things are being handled. Villagers believe that the best way to accomplish a team's goal is to build a consensus among members about what the group aims to achieve and how to do so. As we explained in the preceding chapter, villagers are democratic.

Nonetheless, teams of villagers also take the task at hand very seriously. This is because villagers feel that everyone succeeds or fails together. Like passengers on a boat in a storm, everyone will meet the same fate. If the boat stays afloat, everyone will be safe. If the boat goes down, all on board lose. To villagers, everyone's fate is intertwined. In their minds, it is literally inconceivable that an individual team member could succeed while the team failed. As a result, successfully completing the team's task is of paramount importance.

Getting the job done: what does it take?

If accomplishing the team's goal is so important, it's in everyone's interest for all members of the team to be as strong and as competent as possible. The best strategy for success is to encourage and empower all members of the team as much as possible. If another villager is better at making decisions than you are, it's foolish for

you to do it instead. It would make it harder to get the job done. It's not good for the group. Hence, it's not good for you.

The desire to cultivate the potential of all team members also reinforces the natural proclivity of villagers to focus on developing positive, open and trusting relationships with teammates. For example, villagers want everyone to feel that they can be honest about their strengths and weaknesses. In addition, altruism toward and cooperation among members are vital. With the welfare of the village at stake, selfishness and competitiveness among team members are serious failings. Aggressive, irresponsible, and untrustworthy villagers disrupt positive relationships. Even being perceived as someone who doesn't meet one's responsibilities to the group will earn the rancor of other villagers. Villagers are very tough on this score!

In fact, villagers like equal relationships so strongly, that they distrust villagers who seem to separate themselves from others too much. These villagers are suspected of engaging in self-promotion at the group's expense—even though it may be the case that such a villager is simply trying to help the group achieve its goal.

The members of a team of villagers must also have considerable emotional maturity and expertise. Working on a team is not easy. Even the most compatible villagers will run into disagreements and hard feelings. In addition, the potential for jealousy and envy, the anxiety associated with being candid about one's weaknesses, and the tensions produced by selfish and competitive villagers could produce difficult situations. Therefore, being a successful member of a team of villagers calls for having more than just the technical skills needed to advance the interests of the village. Villagers also need sophisticated emotional skills: abilities to empathize, understand others, communicate, negotiate and resolve conflicts. Otherwise, the harmony of the village is at risk.

A boat in a storm

The image of a 10-person sailboat crew facing a storm in the middle of the ocean captures the way that villagers look at a team. In particular, notice the sorts of things that, when done in the ordinary workings of the boat, increase the odds of everyone on board making it through a crisis.

- *Everyone understands what's important for keeping the boat afloat and has the same agenda.*

- *People on the crew can do many tasks—all very well.* They can tie knots, handle the sails, steer, navigate, operate the radio, fix the motor, save someone who falls over. The more that each person can do, the safer everyone is.

- *People share know-how and responsibilities.* People on board are generous with information about how the boat works and how to perform certain tasks. Villager crewmates aren't possessive or territorial about duties on the boat.

- *The crew works well together.* They are cooperative and helpful. Relationships are harmonious.

- *Personality clashes can be resolved quickly.* Villager crewmates have the interpersonal skills necessary for settling disagreements. And they understand the importance of doing so.

- In a disagreement about how to handle something, *people defer to one another on the basis of expertise, not formal authority.*

- *Egos get left on shore.* People can freely admit that they don't know how to do something or that they need help.

- *No one is punished for telling the truth.* Fixing a problem is more important than assigning blame for it. Everyone on board can comfortably report that there's a problem, even if it's their fault.

If a boat's crew operates this way, it can handle almost any emergency and still make it to land. This is the goal of a team of villagers.

Leadership: who's in charge?

There was little mention of the boat's *captain* in our description of the sailboat at sea. And that brings up another important aspect about villager teams: the question of who's in charge or who's the leader?

The first thing to see about villager teams in this regard, however, is that there is usually no leader! Or perhaps a better way of putting this is that on many villager teams, there's more than one leader. Because villager teams place so much emphasis on expertise, consensus and the good of the village, different team members may come to be regarded by the others as the person to defer to on questions of a certain sort. To the extent that there is a hierarchy on villager teams, it's a fluid one. The person in charge varies depending on the problem at hand.

It is possible, of course, that there may well be a single leader, in the conventional sense, on a team of villagers. If the captain is the obvious leader of the boat, however, it's because he or she is genuinely the most expert person on board. Villager crew members will listen to this person for this reason *only*.

However, the leader of a villager team may not be so obvious as the boat's captain. Such leaders are often low-profile individuals. Thus, it would probably be impossible for outsiders to recognize this individual as the team's leader. And in some cases, even team members might have some trouble doing this. Such a leader may not hold any formal position designating him or her as team leader, boss, department head, chairperson or the like. Yet such leaders have a powerful effect on the actions of other team members. Team members seek them out for help and guidance. Their words are taken very seriously at team meetings. We might say that such leaders have *power*, but not *authority*.

Such leaders have an impact on others by making suggestions, offering words of encouragement, asking helpful questions, guiding the team's discussion of a question or simply musing about how they see some issue. Village leaders often adopt the role of "facilitator." When the discussion is at an impasse, it takes a good judge of character and a skilled diplomat to build consensus and to structure the questions properly so that mutually acceptable options emerge. That is, such leaders don't give orders. (And the fact that they don't have the formal authority to do so is irrelevant. They wouldn't give orders even if they could.) Such leaders also operate more in private and informal settings. And even if the other members of the team wouldn't use the word "leader" to describe this person's role, they would all describe this individual's contribution as invaluable to the team's success.

The villager dilemma

The main difficulties that villagers face when they're on teams, then, lie in a couple of areas. First, villagers have to make sure that focusing so much on process (tending to the relationships among team members, and making sure that everyone is comfortable with the way the team is doing things) doesn't interfere with getting the job done. Second, villagers must be careful that their informal, cooperative style of leadership doesn't degenerate into a situation where the group wastes too much time and lacks direction. The dilemma that villagers face is to strike the proper balance in each of these areas.

Teams of villagers in business

When you put villagers on a team in business, you first find them juggling two things: the task at hand, and the relationships among one another. Accordingly, at the outset of a team's work, villagers may seem to pay more attention to getting along with each other than with getting any work done. If they're supposed to be generating ideas about how to increase the sales of a particular product, for example, they may take a while to get down to business.

Villagers are so sensitive to other people's feelings and to the importance of consensus that they may spend a good deal of time talking just about how to proceed. To the outsider, this may seem like an inefficient way of doing things, if not an absolute waste of time. But it is a very efficient way of building the relationships that the team relies on for its success.

Villagers on a team are cooperative, willing to do necessary but unglamorous work, and they're more comfortable working out of the spotlight. They are usually pretty flexible about what role they'll play on the team, as long as it helps get the job done. They'll make tedious phone calls, write drafts of reports and take minutes at meetings. Villagers will frequently do more than their share of the work, particularly if someone else is running behind in their task.

Villagers tend to shy away from high-profile roles on a team—probably more than they should. Villagers also trust that if someone seeks an important or high-visibility role on the team, it's because that person has the abilities needed to help the group succeed.

Villagers in business put so much emphasis on consensus-building and the will of the group that, if they make a suggestion about how to proceed and it's largely ignored, they assume this means it's a bad idea. Villagers also usually won't press their ideas very hard in the face of opposition or lack of interest, because they're concerned that this will disrupt the harmony of the group.

The leaders of villager teams hang back a lot rather than try to impose their own ideas on the group. Even if villager leaders have a vision about where they want their teams to go, they'll try to develop a consensus about this through gentle suggestions and thoughtful discussion.

Villager leaders will also delegate authority to other members of the group. They will allow team members maximum autonomy and responsibility for their tasks.

When villager leaders have to motivate team members, or if there's a problem that has to be addressed, they'll rely on their relationships with the people on the team. These leaders will talk to the individuals involved, encourage them to be candid, try to understand the situation, communicate their own point of view, and figure out a solution that is mutually acceptable. They won't resort to saying, "Shape up or you're fired."

Villagers try to create a comfortable environment on their team. In order to make sure that no one feels left out, they will openly encourage other team members to share their thoughts. But because villagers don't like to be put on the spot, leaders of villager teams will usually say, "So, does anyone have anything else they want to add?" instead of "So, Roxanne, what do you think about changing the date on which we send out bills?" However, a villager leader's desire to make everyone feel included can lead villagers to discuss someone's ideas far more than they objectively merit.

Warriors: "Winning isn't everything...it's the *only* thing!"

Because warriors and villagers live in different worlds, it should come as no surprise that a *team* means something very different to a warrior. To warriors, everything in life is a contest. And teams are an important way of playing out this competition.

To warriors, a team is first and foremost an instrument for competing. The first order of business on a team of warriors, then, is winning. But don't think that this means just successfully performing the team's task. In order to win, warriors have to prevail in an identifiable game. Warriors see themselves in a contest against other warriors. And the struggle will be conducted according to specific rules.

Moreover, the contest that warriors face by being on a team is complicated by the fact that, whenever warriors are on a team, they actually see themselves involved in two games. There is a group competition against the opposing team. And there's an individual competition against their own teammates.

A football team: games and rules

The way that warriors view teams is roughly the same as what we see in athletics. Accordingly, a football team is more the model of what a team is for warriors than a ship in a storm. And what's involved with being a player on the San Francisco 49ers, for example, is very different from being aboard the *Stenella* when it runs into high winds and rough seas.

To play any game successfully, you have to know the object of the game. So, here, you have to understand what football is all about. You must know your position and know what to do on the different plays. You must also be able to perform the skills required of the game. And you have to know the rules.

But being on a football team automatically puts you in competition against other members of your own team. So that represents the second game that warriors on a team see themselves playing. Let's call this game "stardom." There is an object of the game here as well: making the team, making the first string, becoming a star, perhaps putting yourself in a position to move to a better team. Of course, this game, too, has norms, traditions and rules. And to win in this game, you'd better understand it and know how to play it.

But let's take one game at a time.

Game #1: "Us against them... and the rules"

The members of a football team first see themselves as part of a team playing against another team. In this "game," the success of the team and the success of the individual player are one and the same. No matter how great a game a player has, if the team loses, he or she loses as well.

However, football players (and warriors), are also, we might say, playing against the rules and the officials. A particular foul might be seen by every member of both teams, by thousands of spectators in the stands, and by millions of people watching the game on television. And yet if the official missed it, no foul took place. This means that one

of the unofficial rules of the game in football is that it's okay to try to get away with fouls. In fact, among many athletes, this is considered a skill to be cultivated. Nonathletes (especially villagers) may consider this to be cheating. But to athletes it's all part of the game. Among players, no one is supposed to think there's anything wrong with this or to hold a grudge over an uncalled foul. That's just part of the game.

Similar practices that villager nonathletes may disapprove of, but which some athletes use to improve their chances of winning are things like:

Deception. Pretending that you're hurt when you really aren't might lead an opponent to underestimate you.

Intimidation. Lording any strength or superiority that you have over opponents may shake their confidence. Pushing them around or hitting them with as much as you have in your first encounters may weaken their resolve.

Humiliation. Rolling up as many points as possible against an opponent and trouncing them, not just beating them, can make it easier to defeat other teams that you've yet to face. It can contribute to an image of invincibility.

The unwritten rule involved here is that it's okay to use anything at your disposal to win. As long as you're seen as making a fair move, and not taking a cheap shot at an opponent, there's an understanding among athletes that your actions are in bounds.

Game #2: "Us against *us*"

At the same time that football players are playing against the opposing team, they're also involved in a second game—stardom. But this competition is against members of their own team! And winning in this game is a completely individual matter. All football players vie with one another to be part of the starting lineup and to be a superstar. Being a star, even on a losing team, makes it possible for an athlete to make more money or even to move to a better team. In this game, an "I win, but my team loses" scenario makes perfect sense.

Accordingly, in stardom, players aggressively pursue their own interest, and they must be cautious about helping members of their own team. Helping a teammate competing for the same position could land a player on the bench.

In stardom, then, political skills, savvy and cunning are important strengths. Members of a football team need to be noticed in order to become stars, so they should be masters of self-promotion. And they should always try to create a good impression. No self-respecting football player will ever publicly admit to a weakness, express doubt about whether he can do the job, or suggest that some other player might be a better choice. If anything, players will exaggerate their abilities. They will play when they are injured, for fear that taking themselves out of the game will give an aspiring newcomer the chance to take away their first-string status.

What counts as a foul in the individual competition of stardom? Remember that when you look at the world as a game or contest, something is a foul only if officials call it as such. There are no officials overseeing stardom. So this game can be rough!

Warrior leadership

Being a member of a football team, then, automatically puts players in a situation where they have to juggle these two games. However, it also puts them in a situation where they get to say relatively little about what they'll do during a game. And this brings us to the issue of how warriors view leadership.

Football players are basically told what to do. There is no need for players to build a consensus about how to approach the game. If players step onto the field, they're expected to know what the game is, how to play it and what the rules are. What every player does is determined by which play is called.

It's the quarterback, of course, who calls the plays. The quarterback is the team's leader, who, like a general, orchestrates a strategy aimed at marching his forces down the field to the goal line. The quarterback gets his power as a leader from his position. Whoever has the position, gets to call the plays.

The quarterback is the center of attention and the person in charge. Like the legendary Joe Montana, he's seen as having an almost superhuman ability to motivate and inspire his teammates, and to magically transform defeat into victory. If a quarterback is an effective leader, his vision, decisiveness, daring, charisma and superior athletic abilities allow him to beat impossible odds.

But for this to happen, the leader on the field must have his orders obeyed instantly and without question. And that means that part of such a leader's job is always to project an image of competence and self-assurance to the people following him.

This model of leadership is thus characterized by control of the situation. With the quarterback in charge, it makes no sense to delegate authority to others. Football, like most competitive sports, is built around a military model of organization. So not even the quarterback is king. The quarterback reports to the coach. And on some teams, the coach calls many if not all of the plays. In football, even leaders have to follow orders.

The warrior dilemma

Like football players, warriors find themselves in a complicated situation whenever they're put on teams. They automatically experience themselves as being in a competitive situation—on two fronts. Yet they somehow have to resolve the tensions of the situation. They want to help their team win. But at the same time, warriors need to protect their own interests and to win as individuals—something that may not

happen if they worry too much about what is good for the team.

Yet for all of their independence and autonomy, warriors are, in fact, very much team players. And that only makes their juggling of the two games all the more difficult. They are genuinely torn between helping the team and helping themselves.

Another difficulty warriors on teams face comes from the fact that the ultimate sign of winning at stardom is to become the leader. This prompts many warriors who are actually weak leaders to aspire to a position that they are not fit for. Yet failing to become a leader or doing badly at it condemns them to seeing themselves as lesser warriors, if not outright failures.

Warriors also face difficulties that arise from their preferred style of leadership. First, a decisive and commanding style of leadership may be efficient, but it carries with it a great deal of pressure. Although guiding the team to success will garner great praise for leaders, failure will subject them to an equal amount of blame. Also, it really is "lonely at the top." Warrior leaders are always supposed to know what to do—that's why they're the leaders.

A warrior style of leadership is also tricky to implement. Few people enjoy being told what to do. And warrior leaders like to feel in control. So a commanding style of leadership can build up resentment among some team members. Warrior leaders also face the challenge of learning the difference between decisively guiding the team according to a genuine vision, and impatiently and arrogantly ordering their subordinates around so that the warriors won't look like weak leaders.

Warriors in business

When warriors in business find themselves on a team, they see themselves as being in the same situation as football players. They're trying to beat another team, but they're also trying to beat each other. They want to complete the team project, and they want to advance their own careers. If helping the team achieve its goal will help the warriors individually, then there's no problem. But this isn't always the case. Warriors may think that a particular team project won't help their careers, or they may come to the conclusion that the team is hopelessly off track. At that point, warriors may think that the sensible thing to do is to cut their losses and to put their energies elsewhere—not help the team succeed. With the same logic in mind, warriors try to avoid assignments that amount to doing the team's "scut work." If warriors can't get a visible, high-profile role, they may lose interest.

In business, winning at stardom means being in charge. Thus, on a team of warriors, everyone's basically vying to be the "quarterback." Warriors will try to run team meetings and set the team's strategy. Their version of "leadership" is built on visibility, self-assertion, and self-confidence. Part of winning on a task force is getting everyone

to follow a warrior's lead. When someone else suggests a different strategy, a warrior will naturally resist. Unlike villagers, who are in less conflict about finding the best approach and who have less invested in their own suggestions prevailing, warriors sincerely believe that their ideas are the best. If someone else's idea is better—even if it helps the group do its job—some warriors will still feel that they've lost in the exchange.

Accordingly, team meetings can look like battles. Warriors can compete so much that an objective observer may wonder whether "winning" or getting the job done is the most important priority. Perfectly good ideas are dismissed out of hand by proponents of rival strategies. Many useful recommendations are never even mentioned because the environment is too combative and hostile. And this definitely intimidates the weak-hearted. Warriors sincerely believe that aggressively challenging ideas is the best way to determine their worth. But sometimes this process can look more like "survival of the meanest."

Winning at stardom is so important to warriors in business that virtually all ambitious warriors aim to become managers. After all, that's where the greatest amount of money and power is. The higher they can go, and the more people they can have under them, the better. However, many warriors who have no talent for management still aim to be in charge. And this means that the company as a whole will suffer, and that the people who work for these warriors will probably pay a steep price in terms of their daily peace of mind.

As leaders in business, warriors tend to be controlling. They keep a tight rein on workers. Warrior leaders like to have their directions followed without question or explanation. Leaders of this sort speak of problem employees as "insubordinate" workers who need to be "disciplined." They often motivate workers in a way that demonstrates their power. They'll either promise rewards for good behavior or threaten punishments for bad work.

Warrior leaders keep their cards close to the chest. They generally share information only on a "need to know" basis—even with other members of their team. And they prefer not to delegate tasks or to share authority that they consider their province.

Since any game has rules, how do warriors see the rules of the game in business? One especially important rule is that numbers and dollars are the final word. In the same way that the points on the scoreboard determine which team wins the game, numbers will be taken as the final authority in business as to which strategy is best. Of course, remember that warriors think it's okay to finesse the rules, so they sometimes try to put the "best spin" on some questionable numbers.

The rules of the business game also reward political skills, and they penalize their absence. Candor about one's weaknesses is seen as a serious political error in the minds of warriors, even if it helps the team achieve its end. Self-promotion and visibility are definitely rewarded.

Laura and Paul revisited

It should now be clear, then, what happened between Laura and Paul, the people we met at the beginning of this chapter.

In their first encounter, warrior Paul wanted visibility, and he took advantage of villager Laura's willingness to be marginalized. Laura acted the way villagers naturally do on teams, and she didn't realize that warriors like Paul have a different agenda. Paul didn't manipulate Laura intentionally. He just capitalized on Laura's innocence, good intentions and willingness to help. Of course, as we heard, Laura thinks that Paul has acted in very bad faith. Paul has violated some basic villager taboos. Laura sees him as manipulative and self-centered.

The second episode that Laura complains about stemmed largely from differences in warrior and villager ideas about what an effective leader is like. Laura believes that she's creating a comfortable environment that will lead to the team's getting the job done. Paul is obviously not used to Laura's style, so he thinks there's an absence of leadership on the team. And he moves to fill the void. Of course, Paul's timing for taking over is determined by the fact that his boss shows up. In Paul's version of stardom, he can't pass up the opportunity to impress the coach. Again, both Paul and Laura unfairly draw negative conclusions about each other. Paul sees Laura as a weak leader. In Laura's eyes, Paul doesn't know how to be a team player, needs to be in charge, and is an opportunist.

In the final encounter, Paul decided that it was time to cut his losses—at Laura's expense. He didn't intentionally set her up. It just seemed foolish to him that they should both look bad in front of a boss. Paul didn't plan to sandbag Laura; it just happened. Paul meant it when he said that he'd have expected Laura to do the same if she'd been in his shoes. And he wouldn't have had hard feelings toward Laura. He would have seen it as bad luck on his part and a smart move on hers. Paul thinks he's done nothing wrong, and he's offended by Laura's complaints.

So what do you do?

Okay, warriors and villagers behave differently on teams and as leaders. But what does all of this mean in practical terms? What do you do if you're a villager trying to work with or lead warriors? What do you do if you're a warrior facing the opposite situation?

Advice for villagers

- *Realize just how thoroughly different the experience of being on a "team" is for warriors*

than it is for you. Try this exercise and see if it helps drive the idea home. The next time you're at a meeting at work, visualize the warriors around you in football jerseys and helmets. Even before the meeting gets under way, notice how they'll jostle with each other for position. They'll joke with each other, or maybe they'll put one another down. See them as nervous players who are getting ready to step onto some playing field, and they're trying to tell their competitors that they aren't pushovers. Watch them throughout the meeting through the same eyes. They're trying to score points. They're trying to beat one another out. They act as though everyone else at the meeting—including you—is also wearing a jersey and helmet. They're trying to win because they assume that everyone else has the same goal. This is no doubt very different from how you would describe your own approach to meetings.

- *Recognize and appreciate the advantages of a warrior team.* You may not like the combative atmosphere on a warrior team. And you and the warriors may clash about this. But this doesn't mean that their style lacks value. In fact, a hard-nosed, no-nonsense approach can cut right to the heart of an issue—even though it might bruise egos and feelings. Similarly, demanding that an idea undergo intense scrutiny and stand up to every challenge is perfectly reasonable. The jobs and interests of lots of people are on the line, and these are more important than protecting the feelings of someone who didn't think through an idea fully. In addition, the competition among warriors can push everyone to higher levels of performance. And that's what everybody's getting paid for.

- *Know that if you're on a team of warriors and you act the way you usually do with a team of villagers, you'll be perceived as a "wimp."* If you're surrounded by hardcore warriors, you should probably think about adopting a more assertive style in dealing with them. If you wait for your turn to speak, fail to aggressively defend your ideas, avoid sharp disagreements, and are overly cooperative, you will be seen as weak by your warrior teammates. And no one respects weakness.

- *Don't take it personally.* If you're a villager on a team of warriors, know that the warriors aren't out to give you a hard time. This is just the way warriors deal with the world. There's no malice involved. Warriors aren't treating you any differently from anyone else. They just assume that everyone else is a warrior like themselves and is going to play the game. Knowing at the outset that this isn't personal should at least lessen any feelings that you may have of being attacked. And it will also reduce the likelihood that you'll react defensively.

- *Realize that you're in a situation involving two games: the group project and competition among individuals.* Individual competition with teammates may make no sense to you, but it's going to go on among warriors. This means that warriors will vie for being in charge. Be careful not to let anyone convince you to be a cheerleader, water boy or benchwarmer under the guise of helping the team.

What can you do? Try to get the less glamorous work shared by everyone on the team. Or, if the work of a task force is going to go on for a while, suggest that roles on the team rotate. Laura could have suggested that she and Paul share the research.

She could have found out the competitors' prices and suggested that Paul handle the first-year sales projections. They could have formulated the recommendations jointly. And they each could have done a piece of the presentation.

- *Take the initiative to set a positive, cooperative, supportive environment for your team.* Praise your teammates. Spread any credit around. Do not dwell unnecessarily on mistakes people make. This will often make warriors feel more comfortable because you appear to be less of a head-on competitor. You're also making them feel like they're winning— even if no one else is losing. Warriors generally feel that anyone willing to make them look good is an ally rather than an adversary. They then tend to be a little more cooperative.

- *Suggest that meetings take place in informal rather than formal settings.* In particular, avoid long tables with a head. If you can, arrange the furniture in a circle or in a U-shape. Informal, egalitarian arrangements make some warriors feel more relaxed and cooperative. They feel less like they're in the middle of the "big game" against their main rival and more like they're on a local

practice field with friends. This also makes it harder for warriors to plant themselves in power positions at the table and exercise influence simply by virtue of their location.

- *If you feel that the work of your team isn't going well when you all get together, work as much as you can with your teammates individually.* Talk to people separately about your ideas before a group meeting. Recognize that different warriors have different interests. Try to identify them ahead of time. In particular, try to determine what will genuinely advance everyone's interests. Sometimes warriors get so involved in winning that they actually fail to advance their own interests. Take the lead in getting to know what's important to everyone else on your team so that you can begin fashioning a win-win scenario.

- *Be careful not to be blindsided.* Remember that in stardom, there's no official to call fouls. You may be facing a situation in which anything goes. Be particularly careful about protecting your ideas. Unscrupulous warriors treat a good idea like a fumbled football—they pick it up and try to score points with it. Put as much as you can in writing. Send memos to members of your department, your boss and your boss's bosses in which you outline your suggestions. There will then be little question where the ideas came from. Memos are a great tool for self-promotion if you're uncomfortable putting yourself in the limelight.

- *If you make a suggestion at a meeting and it's ignored, don't assume that it's a bad idea.* In fact, this may be a sign that it's better than anything any of the warriors have come up with. A couple of favorite ways that warriors have of responding to a good idea from a competitor is to ignore it or to rephrase it so that it sounds trivial. Remember, a conference table is a playing field for a warrior, and a warrior will always resist the attempt of someone else to call the plays. Act accordingly. Don't let your ideas be misrepresented. Repeat. Reiterate. Clarify. Elaborate until they're seen for what they are. And keep pushing an idea until *you're* convinced that it's a bad idea.

- *Recognize the power connected with volunteering to write the follow-up memo for a meeting or the report of a task*

force. Don't make the mistake of seeing this just as secretarial work. This may actually give you some clout in making sure that the work of the group is evenly divided: "I'd like a couple pages from everyone summarizing a different aspect of our decision. Frank, will you do the first product we discussed? Ruth, the second? George, the third? And I'll do the last one." Also, if you're convinced that the group erred by ignoring your ideas, you can go back to them and say that after reviewing your notes for the report, you think the group is making a serious mistake. This will give you another chance to make your case and ensure that the group does the best job possible. And consider approaching team members individually, rather than as a group. This might give you a better hearing.

- *Be aware that warriors compete even when it comes to being heard at a meeting.* Warriors usually don't hesitate to interrupt one another. Be prepared for this. Let the interrupter know—clearly and firmly—that you haven't finished speaking yet. Some people cope with the problem of being heard at meetings by deliberately speaking softly, thus making everyone pay attention.

- *Use to your advantage the fact that the rules of the game in business dictate that the bottom line is the final word.* Warriors have to listen to numbers, even when they don't want to.

- *But remember that warriors think it's okay to finesse the rules.* This means they may sometimes try to "massage" the numbers to their own advantage. Be on the lookout for this. If a warrior's numbers feel wrong, they probably are. Trust your instincts, and don't be buffaloed.

- *Get noticed.* As difficult as it may be for you, try to get comfortable being the center of attention. Speak up at meetings. Develop good platform skills. Send memos. Keep your name in front of the people who matter. See yourself as a product that no one but you is going to market. Never turn down a project, even if it's something you think you aren't that good at. Look at it as a way to learn something new.

- *Even a small role is better than none.* Even if you're uncomfortable doing presentations and prefer to let someone else on your team take the lead, be sure to be part of the question-and-answer session. By answering questions, you'll let other people see how smart you are.

- *Be visible, but watch how far out on a limb you're going.* The mistake Laura made was that she let herself become too vulnerable. Be prudent. If, like Laura, you don't know how your ideas will be accepted, and you fear that the warriors on your team will jump ship, be sure to spread around ownership of the ideas.

- *Be aware that a team of warriors isn't a democracy.* The rules of the game among warriors are lead, follow or get out of the way. If your natural strategies for persuading people fail, you have few options. You must either convince the guy in charge or find a way to best everyone else.

- *Don't try to beat warriors at their own game unless you're committed to adopting this as a new way of life.* You can't be a warrior just for a day. If you decide to deal with hard-core warriors on their own terms, realize that they'll now see you as being willing to play by their rules. In particular, don't start an encounter with warriors by trying to "win" and then change your mind. Your warrior opponents won't believe you. They'll think your change of heart is a stratagem that you've adopted because you found that you couldn't beat them head on. Be prepared for them to be deceptive. They'll only be trying to match what they take as your strategy. So don't "declare war" in the first place.

- *Do not distrust warriors who want to be in the spotlight.* They are not necessarily self-promoters. They may be as interested as you are in having the team do the best job possible. These people can marshall support for an idea that you probably can't. Such warriors can also be invaluable when the team gets to the point of having to "sell" its conclusions or recommendations to your final audience.

- *If you're trying to motivate a warrior, you might have to use tactics that you—but not the warrior—are uncomfortable with.*

Betsy, a villager manager, was having trouble with David, one of the warriors on her sales team. At David's quarterly review, Betsy explained that he was the only member of the team below quota, and she asked what she could do to help boost his performance.

Did he need additional support? Would receiving extra training or attending a workshop on selling help?

At David's next review, the situation was unchanged. This time Betsy asked whether any personal problems were affecting his job. Were his customers being unusually resistant? Did he think he had a bad territory? Again, how could she help?

When David came in for his next review, Betsy was having a terrible day. Her car broke down. There were rumors of layoffs. She'd had a run-in with her boss. By the time she met with David, she was out of patience. "Look," she said with exasperation, "I don't know what the problem is, but I don't care. Get your numbers up or you're fired! Now get out of here and get back to work." Startled, David left the office. In the following weeks, guilt over how she had handled David gnawed away at Betsy. She had never spoken to an employee like that. She prided herself on being helpful and supportive. She was embarrassed that she'd let her own troubles get to her as they did, and she was ashamed that she'd threatened a subordinate. She resolved to apologize to David the next time she saw him.

The only problem was that as the quarter progressed, David's performance improved dramatically. As Betsy reviewed her conversations with David, she realized that until she said that David's job was in jeopardy, she had not communicated effectively to David that he was on the verge of losing in a big way. And David's feelings were not hurt by the threat. As long as he knew the score, he was happy. As a warrior, he knew that Betsy's comment wasn't motivated by anything personal. And until Betsy threatened to use her power over David, he assumed that his falling short wasn't really all that important to her.

Betsy is still unhappy with how she handled the situation. But now what she feels guilty about is that she let David go for so long without an adequate understanding of the risks he was running. She learned that some warriors would listen to her only when she spoke to them as another warrior would.

- *If you're trying to convince your warrior boss of an idea, try "diplomacy by fiction."* In this strategy, you set aside your own ego and appeal to the warrior desire to look capable and powerful. Attribute the genesis of your idea to the warrior: "I was thinking about what you said the other day, and I was wondering if something like this is what you had in mind." Link the idea to the warrior's self-image: "What I especially like about this idea is that it shows how concerned this department is with fairness, and I know how important that is to you." Give away the credit: "I think your decision

about how to handle this problem is great." You get the idea.

Advice for warriors

Likewise, what do you do if you're a warrior trying to work with or lead villagers?

- *Realize just how thoroughly different the experience of being on a team is for villagers than it is for you.* The next time you're at a meeting at work, imagine the villagers around you as the crew members of a boat that's heading for stormy seas. See everything they do as aiming at learning about one another and making sure that everyone will be willing to help one another once the storm hits. They aren't "gossiping"; they're sharing stories and finding out what kind of "mates" they're sailing with. They aren't afraid to criticize each other's ideas; they're ensuring that no one will be afraid to say, "I'm sorry, but I just threw the anchor overboard." They say, "I think Alicia would do a better job of presenting than I would" not because they don't have the nerve to be in the spotlight; they want to make sure that everyone on board can navigate the boat or tie knots.

- *Recognize and appreciate the advantages of a villager team.* The atmosphere may seem unbusinesslike and inefficient. And you may feel like you're having to walk on eggs so that you don't bruise anyone's feelings. But recognize how well villagers can work together when they don't feel competitive toward each other. They're helpful and trustful. They go the extra mile without worrying what's in it for them as individuals. The friendly tone of meetings lets some people who are normally reticent about talking in groups make some valuable suggestions. And concentrating on what's good in an idea, instead of what's wrong with it, gives them more useful possibilities from which to choose in trying to solve a problem.

- *If you act the way you usually do on a team of warriors, you're going to be perceived as an aggressive, self-serving barbarian.* If you're surrounded by villagers, you might consider trying to tone down some of your actions. Be careful that you don't do anything that will make you look like you're putting the "boat" in jeopardy just to look good. Some warriors may think that you'd have to be an idiot to volunteer to do the necessary, but unglamorous, work on a team. But villagers take this as a sure sign of good faith.

When your team gets to the point of deciding how all of you will present your results or recommendations, know that the group wants to find the best person for the job. If the question "Who's really good on their feet?" is asked, don't say that you are unless it's true. Otherwise, your villager teammates will be angry and resentful at what they'll take as your being self-serving.

- *Be aware of the fact that villagers consider juggling task and relationship to be part of the responsibilities of a villager team-member.* If you don't tend to relationships as well as tend to business, you won't be seen as a committed member of the group by your villager teammates.

- *Don't underestimate the villagers on your team.* This is probably a warrior's biggest mistake when dealing with villagers. Don't mistake cooperativeness with being spineless or having no mind of one's own. Don't mistake silence with incompetence. Don't write off people who don't want to be in the spotlight.

At one company with a warrior culture, a villager named Anya quietly worked long hours. Hoping for an opportunity to become a manager, Anya be-lieved that being dependable and effective would guarantee a promotion. One day, however, she overheard a superior say that she would never go anywhere in the company because she was so "unambitious." What he was responding to was the fact that Anya engaged in less self-promotion than many of her warrior colleagues. Because Anya was, in fact, ambitious, she left the company. And the firm lost a solid employee and a promising manager.

- *To be an effective leader with villagers, minimize the distance between you and them.* Don't pretend that you have no weaknesses, as warriors often do. Reveal something about yourself—hopes, dreams, concerns. It need not be deeply personal, but it should put a human face on you. Villagers feel connected to other *people*, not *managers* or *teammates*.

- *As a leader, try not to order villagers around—even though you have the authority to do so.* If you let villagers who work for you feel that they are part of the process that determines the shape of their lives, they will work harder than if they feel that they are simply doing your bidding.

- *Give up the warrior mask of omniscience and omnipotence.* Villagers will respect you more, not less, if you admit that you don't know everything and that you can genuinely use their help.

- *To convince villagers, talk about the human impact of what you want them to do.* As a leader, talk about *people*, not rules, policies, numbers or the bottom line. It is always possible to link the numbers of business to someone: customers, employees, vendors, etc.

Different teams, different leaders

Given what we saw in the first two chapters of this book about the profound differences between the way that warriors and villagers experience life in general and in how they think about business, it's not surprising that they'd see teams and leaders so differently. The differences are extensive.

Villager teams

- Are always trying to balance accomplishing the team's task with developing positive relationships among team members.

- Emphasize cooperation, consensus and empowering team members.

- See the success of the group and the success of individual team members as being identical.

- Value open and candid communication about individual strengths and weaknesses.

- Expect altruism among their members.

- Regard competitiveness and self-promotion as weaknesses.

- Require team members to have considerable emotional skills.

- Determine transgressions according to the perception of other members of the team.

Villager leaders

- Are low-profile individuals.

- Work at establishing a sense of equality with the people who work for them.

- Prefer to lead through extensive team discussion, "buy-in" and consensus-building.

- Readily delegate authority and responsibility to others.

Warrior teams

- Are always involved in two games: one deals with the task at hand, the other concerns

competition among individuals on the team.

- See the success of the group and the success of the individual not as intertwined as villagers do.

- Decide what to do according to authority, rules and the competition for influence.

- Value political skills in advancing one's private interests.

- See self-promotion as a strength.

- Regard candor about one's private strategy and, especially, about one's limitations, as weaknesses.

- Consider something a transgression only when it's called so by an "official," and sees getting away with fouls as a virtue.

Warrior leaders

- Like to be seen as highly visible, out in front, charismatic and visionary individuals.

- Prefer to be thought of as *above* their subordinates.

- Are comfortable using their formal authority and issuing orders to subordinates.

- Expect their orders to be obeyed without question or explanation.

- Often motivate through rewards and punishments.

Strengths and weaknesses: mistaken perceptions

Warriors and villagers have such different ideas about teams and leaders that they are almost diametrically opposed.

Indeed, what warriors count as strengths, villagers see as weaknesses, and vice versa. Not recognizing these differences leads to serious consequences. First, warriors and villagers on the same team will obviously be operating at cross-purposes. The team will not work well together. And the final product will surely not be as good as it could have been.

In addition, being on the opposite team can be disastrous for warriors and villagers alike. Villagers on a team of warriors will be easy marks because they will be perceived as weak. Villagers may give advice or make suggestions that let rival warriors come out on top. Villagers may be candid about their fears and weaknesses, and this information may be used against them.

Warriors on a team of villagers will be perceived as aggressive, domineering and self-serving. The warriors will no doubt be the target of a good deal of concealed hostility from the villagers. And some villager teammates may try to remove the warriors from the group.

It's the same story when we talk about leaders. In the eyes of villagers, warrior leaders are Napoleonic "control freaks" who think they're in the army rather than in business. Villagers think that warrior leaders believe that they're better than the people who work for them. Villagers see them as cold and distant people who hide behind their job title and treat their employees like children.

Warriors see villager leaders as weak, chaotic, soft-headed, and unbusinesslike. Warriors think that these villagers have forgotten that they're bosses and act like they're camp counselors. Warriors think that the villager emphasis on consensus and empowerment stems from an insatiable need to be liked.

As we stated at the outset of this book, however, the perceptions of both warriors and villagers are wrong. Warriors and villagers are different. But that's all—different. Their respective ideas about teams and leaders have strengths and weaknesses. But neither is right and neither is wrong.

Chapter Four

Working against one another

As the two executives walked out of the meeting, Vicki turned to Jarod and said, "God, that was the proverbial 'meeting from Hell.' I've got to get out of here for a while. Do you want to go out for lunch?"

"Absolutely," her colleague replied. "Those people made me crazy. What went on in there?"

"As far as I can figure, everyone's buttons got pushed at the same meeting, and then we took it out on each other," observed Vicki as they stepped out of the building. "To be honest, mine got pushed even before we got started. As soon as I walked in, Bill made a big deal about my being top performer this quarter. He was sure he was going to win. But a deal came through at the last minute, and I nosed him out. He just wouldn't let up: 'All rise! Madam Hot Shot's here! Enjoy it while you can, because that's the last time I'm letting you win. So how much did you have to kick back for that last deal?' I didn't know what to say. What does he want me to do? Apologize? That stuff really bothers me. And once the meeting began, Bill kept it up by jumping all over me anytime I said anything. I felt that as soon as I finished talking, he had to prove me wrong. That guy really had it in for me today."

"Well, you know Bill: 'slash and burn.' He doesn't mean anything by it. That's the way he is with everybody. Don't let him get to you," advised Jarod.

"Right, just like you didn't let Gloria bother you?" observed Vicki. "You looked like you wanted to slug her."

"That's different," explained Jarod. "I wouldn't lobby with my boss to try to get Gloria transferred into our section, and now she's making me pay for it. Last week, she kept me waiting for a half-hour before she'd see me. Every time I call, she's 'in a meeting.' And the latest thing she did was to *forget* to make the slides for my presentation tomorrow. She said *maybe* she can have them ready this afternoon. I hate being jerked around like this. But every time I ask Gloria if she's mad at me, she says, 'No, everything's fine.' I'm furious that's she's being two-faced. I'd rather be in Corinne's situation. At least I'd know how to handle that."

"What do you mean?" asked Vicki.

"Didn't you notice how Helen really got Corinne on edge?" Jarod continued. "Helen's a 'toucher.' Corinne hates people touching her, but she never knows how to tell people that it bothers her. That's why after a few minutes Corinne said she had to go check with her assistant about something. She just wanted to find a way to sit someplace else without being too obvious about it. I know it killed her to walk back in and find that the only empty seat was the one beside Helen."

"I wondered why she squirmed in her chair so much and was so short with everybody," said Vicki.

"And then what happened when Cindy and Anne cornered you just now?" asked Jarod. "I thought you guys were tight, but they were really mad at you at the end of the meeting. And you still seem upset."

"I am," explained Vicki. "They're angry that I spoke against establishing a day-care center on site. They see this as a woman's issue, and they've been pressuring me to support the idea. They think that all the women should stick together on this one. As an accountant, I just don't see how the company can afford it yet, but I still feel guilty. They've made me feel that I'm disloyal and that I've betrayed my friendship with them. What they said really hurt. I'm afraid that it's going to ruin everything between us."

"I'm really sorry about that," replied Jarod sympathetically. "Oh well, let's just have lunch and plot revenge."

....

Aggression and vulnerability: we're all alike

Like it or not, deliberately or not, we all regularly give one another a hard time. It's simply a fact of human nature that all of us can hurt and can be hurt by each other.

For openers, we all have an ambitious and aggressive side to our personality. With some of us, it's out in the open. With others, it's concealed. Sometimes this comes out in what we do, other times in what we say. But, warriors and villagers alike, we're all assertive or aggressive in one way or another.

There's nothing inherently wrong with aggression. Millions of years on this planet have taught us that in order to get what we need, we have to push to overcome obstacles. Sometimes it's a force of nature. Sometimes it's the challenge of a difficult task. Sometimes we struggle against each other. But unless we regularly take strong, assertive actions, we will never get what we want.

The major drawback to our being ambitious, aggressive or assertive, of course, is that it exists in tandem with our vulnerability. Warriors and villagers alike can be hurt by what other people say and do. Our aggression is especially problematic when it's driven by hostility and used to deliberately hurt someone. However, even when we don't intend it, our assertive actions and angry words can wound. A co-worker's drive to be vice president by the time he or she is 30, can feel like it leaves cleat marks on your back. A thoughtless, irate comment to your secretary can make him or her perceive you as a threat.

(You might be uneasy about the term "aggressive," because, in your mind, it may mean trying to hurt someone else. You may see "aggression" as always negative and distinguish it from "assertiveness." In this chapter, however, we're going to use "aggression" to refer to a basic—but not necessarily harmful—impulse that we harness whenever we push against one another to achieve our goals. From this point of view, athletes on a playing field or a group of people in a sales competition are being aggressive in their drive to win. We'll use "hostility" to refer to negative aggression—that is, aggression that aims to hurt someone.)

Aggression and vulnerability: we're also different

Yet as much as warriors and villagers are the same in being assertive or aggressive, on the one hand, and

vulnerable, on the other, their opposing psychologies produce some major differences between them. Warriors and villagers "push" differently—especially when it comes to pushing against other people. Similarly, different things make warriors and villagers feel threatened and intimidated. Some behaviors that warriors see as normal and friendly feel hostile to villagers. Likewise, some amicable villager actions feel hostile to warriors. And because warriors and villagers are largely unaware of these differences, this is yet another area where people misunderstand each other on the job.

The result: unintentionally giving one another a hard time

This chapter is about how the differences in how warriors and villagers are aggressive and vulnerable lead them, unintentionally, to make the workplace feel uncomfortable—even hostile. But even if accidental, giving one another a hard time can have a dramatic effect on how people feel about where they work and, thus, how well they do their jobs.

We'll start by describing the differences in how warriors and villagers are aggressive and vulnerable. We'll see how this produces problems in the workplace. We'll talk about ways to handle these situations. And then we'll return to our opening dilemmas.

Warriors just naturally stab

Warriors and villagers are, in reality, equally assertive and aggressive.

However, the way that warriors "push" is easier to see. After all, warriors live daily on a battlefield where they vie against other warriors. Pushing against other warriors is simply a fact of life. "Stabbing" at each other is normal and expected—indeed, it's absolutely necessary—if a warrior is going to succeed in life's contest. Warriors have no moral qualms about aggression. In fact, they see it as a virtue and a sign of strength.

Warrior ambition and aggression are also readily visible because they're usually right out in the open. Warriors are so comfortable competing head-to-head against other warriors—on a playing field or in the workplace—that they see no reason to conceal it. They openly criticize, issue challenges and taunt one another. Warriors are at ease with publicly pressuring other warriors, pushing them around psychologically, and being pushed back by them. Indeed, many warriors revel in this process because they find that battling against a strong opponent often motivates them to turn in a superior performance. Driving themselves to best someone else in a public competition is the secret to their success.

Warriors and aggression: it's varied

Aggression and competition among warriors take many forms. Sometimes it's in earnest. Only one person can run the department or win a sales contest, for example. So the contending warriors

conduct the bout with all the intensity of a fight to the death.

Sometimes, warrior aggressiveness surfaces in someone's being argumentative. Many warriors test ideas—their own and other people's—through a kind of ritual intellectual combat. They believe that if an idea is any good, it will stand up to intense scrutiny from every conceivable angle. Accordingly, they will defend their own ideas with a single-minded passion, and they'll relentlessly challenge other people's ideas. When warriors are in this mode, it may look like they can't take criticism and that ego is the only thing they care about. And the verve of their attack on someone else's ideas may look like it's personally motivated. However, being argumentative is simply a common way that many warriors "push" in doing business.

There are even times when warrior aggressiveness is almost a game. That is, it's more like friendly sparring than anything serious. Notice the verbal banter that takes place when warriors first get together. Warriors nearly always begin their encounters by kidding or needling one another, by coming up with friendly put-downs, and by trying to top one another with clever comebacks. In effect, warriors stand around and insult one another for sport, the way they do at a "roast." Warriors who fail to come up with snappy comebacks or who show they are stung by the remarks and get angry, "lose" in the exchange. But it's still mainly a game.

Aggression, not hostility

No matter what form warrior "pushing" takes, however, it's important to see that warriors normally don't take it personally. As the saying goes, "It's just business; it's nothing personal."

Warriors are competitive and aggressive, then, but not usually hostile. If a warrior loses a sale or a promotion to someone else, he or she will obviously be disappointed. But warriors generally don't feel that the victor deliberately set out to inflict personal harm on them. As long as the competition has been fair, warriors don't bear grudges, and they don't try to settle personal scores. A strong desire to win may make them move the contest to another arena—for example, after losing out as "employee of the month," a warrior may immediately start a "rematch" with the victor in the next month's competition. But refusing to lose doesn't mean they attribute malice to those who beat them.

Similarly, warriors don't take offense at the barbs thrown around in verbal dueling. Indeed, the mutual insults are often a kind of ritual bonding in which warriors show their acceptance of one another and prove that they belong in the group. The sparring lets them show that they're clever enough to dish it out and tough enough to take it.

Warriors stab—but they also wear armor

Warriors have a fairly thick skin because they come to the contest fully prepared. They arrive with weapons to use against other warriors. They don't see another warrior's actions as personal hostility. They are prepared for the fact that other warriors will do the same. And to protect themselves, they carry "shields" and wear "armor." That is, they have psychological defenses that protect them from being hurt by most of the "stabbing" by other warriors. Armor that is sufficiently strong will allow a warrior to come out of a serious conflict with another warrior totally unscathed. Warrior armor is also what keeps warriors from taking offense at the daily hassling they get from others.

Wearing armor, however, does have drawbacks. Unusually impenetrable armor has been known to produce warriors with a high tolerance for anger and hostility. Sometimes this tolerance is so high that they act as though it's impossible for their own or anyone else's aggression to genuinely hurt anybody.

Similarly, this psychological armor can lead some warriors to completely ignore other people's threats and warnings. Such warriors believe that angry or aggressive language is easy and empty—"just words." And they pay attention to an adversary only when he or she takes some aggressive action. Thus, they may inadvertently provoke a conflict that could have been avoided.

Warrior vulnerability

Of course, warriors come to the battlefield armed and protected because, being human, they're vulnerable to being hurt. Warriors may appear to revel in head-to-head competition, but that doesn't mean that losing in a high-stakes contest won't wound them. Warriors may seem thick-skinned while engaging in verbal banter without flinching, but that doesn't mean that every insult actually bounces off.

One of the difficulties of reading warriors is that part of their required "armor" is the ability to conceal from other warriors that they're hurt. In life's great contest, letting other warriors know how you can be injured puts you at a major disadvantage. Any sign of vulnerability or of an unprotected flank is read by other warriors as a weakness, and this information is filed away in the back of their minds for future use. As a result, warriors logically try to conceal their vulnerability.

Still, warriors do get hurt—by other warriors and by villagers. So in order to keep the workplace comfortable for everyone, it's important to know where a warrior's vulnerabilities are and how to avoid inadvertently wounding a warrior.

Warrior vulnerabilities: being controlled, being smothered

So what are a warrior's vulnerabilities? Warriors feel threatened mainly when other people jeopardize their autonomy and independence. Nothing makes a warrior feel worse than being stripped of weapons and armor and being completely under the thumb of an adversary. A warrior's worst nightmare is being controlled and pushed around.

But warriors can also feel unsettled if they feel that someone is getting too close. The closer an enemy is, the easier it will be for him or her to mortally wound a warrior. Stepping into someone's "personal space" is taken as a sign of aggression by warriors in our culture. Therefore, the most clever enemies will get close by deception—offering friendship or love as a way of getting the warrior to let down his or her guard.

Even closeness with friends can be problematic. Having the arms of a loved one wrapped tightly around a warrior makes it harder for him or her to respond to a threat. In short, closeness may feel threatening or smothering.

Warriors, then, can read a variety of things as either aggressive or threatening: a direct challenge, something that smacks of duplicity, even personal closeness.

Villager aggression: it feels uncomfortable

Villager "pushing" differs dramatically from warrior "pushing." And this is largely because villagers feel less comfortable than warriors do being assertive and aggressive. Remember that villagers experience the world as a community, not a contest. Getting along with one another, not defeating one another, is their most important priority. So anything that jeopardizes the harmony of the group or that can ruin a relationship, as aggression obviously can, becomes highly problematic—even dangerous—in a villager's eyes.

To be openly ambitious, competitive or aggressive is profoundly unacceptable among villagers. It violates a core taboo against placing your own interest ahead of the village's. It marks a villager as untrustworthy and selfish—someone other villagers will not necessarily be able to count on for help in a crisis. There is such a strong prohibition against being outwardly aggressive and competitive that acting this way generally evokes no small amount of guilt among villagers.

Aggression without guilt

The taboo against open aggression, however, doesn't change the fact that villagers have as many aggressive feelings as warriors do. Villagers are no different from warriors in being ambitious, in getting angry when they're thwarted, in wanting to thwart competitors, and in wanting to take action against adversaries. But the village taboo makes it difficult for villagers to express these feelings without feeling guilty. In essence, villagers need a way to be aggressive without appearing to be so—either to others or to themselves. This lets them observe the traditions of the "village" and also keep their own image of themselves as "good" villagers.

Villager "pushing"

Villager ambition is less openly competitive than warrior ambition. For good or ill, villagers believe that success in business comes from other people recognizing that you're doing a job well, not from beating someone else out for limited opportunities. Thus, in the normal course of their jobs, villagers tend to "push" less against competitors than warriors do.

Villagers will "push" against others when they feel aggrieved. This is where they can make life difficult for warriors, because villager aggression is generally more covert, private, psychological or indirect than warrior aggression. And that makes it harder to see.

Villager sabotage: indirect aggression

Villagers live on the horns of a dilemma. They want to be able to compete aggressively in business while at the same time preserving the appearance of outward peace and group harmony. An angry villager may fume in silence when someone else claims the credit after the villager has figured out how to get a project back on schedule. But the public expression of these feelings can't be obvious. As a result, villagers often try to deal with competitors by acting aggressively toward them in an indirect way.

A classic way that aggression surfaces is for the villager to become quietly uncooperative. For example, a villager may begin to arrive late at meetings or to miss them altogether, to turn in reports late without warning or explanation, to be remiss about returning phone calls, to "forget" to do certain tasks, to fail to keep a variety of commitments, to ignore direct requests, or to decide not to keep enemies informed about things that affect them. (A favorite bit of villager aggression of this sort is not to tell the person they're annoyed with about problems that are developing on a project that he or she is ultimately responsible for. The news is delivered only when it's too late to set things right, so the villager's victim is left "holding the bag.")

The point of this style of aggression is to make someone's life difficult without revealing that that's what the villager is doing. In fact, villagers who engage in indirect aggression normally are, in public, quite friendly with the people they're trying to sabotage.

Villager sabotage: enlisting others

Villager aggression may also be involved when villagers choose to blow off steam to friends instead of confronting an opponent directly. To some extent, of course, this may be an innocent way of getting emotional support. However, this behavior crosses the line into aggression if a villager is actually trying to enlist others in a campaign to undermine someone. Villagers may hope that their complaint will lead friends to act negatively towards their adversary: to badmouth him or her to bosses and co-workers, to delay answering requests, perhaps even to misfile something important. Villagers may even explicitly ask friends to do these

things. The object is minimally to make an opponent's days more annoying. But the villager usually hopes for more— that it will hurt an opponent's reputation and performance.

This kind of aggression can even extend to trying to enlist an enemy's own friends and associates. Angry villagers may try to develop their own competing relationships with these people. Or they may engage in a series of private conversations in which they use the pretext of asking for advice as a way of disparaging someone: "You've known Ken for years. Perhaps you can help me understand why he's treating me so badly," or "You and Claire are friends. What do you think I should do to get her to stop criticizing my work?" In reality, the point of the conversation is to present themselves as an innocent victim in need of help. By approaching this way, a villager aims to challenge and confuse the friends' loyalty and allegiance. This sabotages an enemy by undermining and weakening his or her network of supporters.

Once again, however, outward harmony and a "good villager" image are preserved. The aggression is concealed. It's even masked by the claim that the villager is just looking for friendship or help with a problem.

Villagers are guerrillas—but don't want to admit it

You may be surprised and somewhat unsettled by this account of villager "pushing"—particularly if you're a villager. You may feel uneasy about the indirect, duplicitous and manipulative character of villager aggression. And you may feel that this doesn't square with the idea that harmony and cooperation are important to villagers.

Remember, however, that aggression is a natural, human trait. What this style of aggression reveals, then, is simply that, given their psychology, villagers are more comfortable fighting like *guerrillas.*

The fact that villagers are guerrillas probably makes them more dangerous than most people think. However, what also makes them dangerous is that most villagers are deeply offended by being characterized this way. They would, with great sincerity, simply deny that they plot against other people. However, for villagers to deny their own aggression is to refuse to see the harm that comes from what they do. And this is a very serious consequence of the village taboo against open conflict and a major problem that accompanies villager aggression. Some villagers may thus be as oblivious to the harm they do as are warriors with impenetrable armor.

Words are weapons

The village taboo against open aggression also means that villagers don't carry weapons, as warriors do. (It's as much a cardinal rule among villagers never to carry swords as it is among warriors never to be without one.) But if villagers want to combat an adversary, they need to use something. And what do they rely on? Words.

Notice how the villager strategy of undermining someone is largely verbal. Villagers *talk* to their friends or they *talk* to their opponent's friends. And remember that villagers typically use *friendly words* to cloak their indirect aggression against someone.

When villagers finally engage in direct conflict with an adversary, they express themselves more with words than with actions. They seek out a private conversation with someone rather than, say, arrange for a public "showdown" at a meeting in which they've already "stacked the deck" against an opponent.

Villagers rely so strongly on words because they're very effective in the "village." Keep in mind just how important maintaining cooperative relationships is for villagers. Because so much depends on keeping relationships on an even keel, villagers try to be sensitive to any signs of anger from other villagers. After all, the more unhappy one villager is with another, the less likely it is that that villager will come to the other's aid in a time of need. What villagers say to one another is a barometer of the state of the relationship between them. So they take words very seriously. Even a simple remark like, "I no longer feel comfortable working together," can feel like a punch to the stomach.

Villager vulnerabilities: villagers don't wear armor

Villager psychology and village taboos may make it difficult to root out villager aggression, but they make it relatively easy to identify ways that villagers are most vulnerable to being hurt or to feeling threatened.

The most obvious reason for villagers' vulnerabilities is that, unlike warriors, villagers don't wear the psychological "armor" that warriors do. They don't wear armor for the same reason that they don't carry weapons. This would get in the way of developing open, trusting, close relationships with other villagers.

However, not wearing armor does produce a heightened sense of vulnerability in villagers. Living without armor means that almost anything—words, looks, jokes, taunts—can sting a villager. Comments that "bounce off" warriors can feel like barbs to villagers. Living without armor also means that villagers are especially aware of how dangerous an unscrupulous villager could be.

Villager vulnerabilities: a wolf within the flock

Discovering that someone in the village preys on other villagers is a villager's worst nightmare. A villager's whole world is based on the desire to trust, to be open and to connect with other people. Villagers' main strengths, then, make them easy to take advantage of. A predator in the village will have an easy time finding victims, and villagers know that. Villagers also know that unscrupulous villagers are clever. On the surface, they are charming, endearing, disarming and vulnerable. They may even seem wounded and in need of someone to care for them.

But these people are masters of deception. And they don't show their true colors until their victim has let them get close, and it's too late. Moreover, villagers know that some predators are so expert at their craft that they can even make their victims feel responsible for being victimized. Victims come to feel that their aggressor's predatory nature is less to blame than their own trusting nature. Indeed, instead of feeling angry at being victimized by someone they trusted, villagers may feel guilty, ashamed, humiliated and stupid for being deceived.

In essence, the combination of villager psychology and the absence of armor leaves villagers vulnerable to being hurt in a particularly pernicious way by the "wolf in the flock." First, they are victimized. (Let's say someone steals an idea.) Then, they're victimized a second time by their aggressor's reaction to being caught. Predators may try to minimize the seriousness of what they did—something that makes victims question the legitimacy of their own feelings of being hurt. ("Come on, you have great ideas all the time, and the boss likes you. I could tell that if I didn't impress Ramon soon, I was going to be history. Hey, it saved my job.")

Or they may shift the blame to the victim by, in essence, assaulting their sanity. A predator may look a victim right in the eye and flatly deny what he or she did. ("I don't care what Chuck said, I didn't tell Ramon it was my idea. And I'm really hurt that you'd think I could do something like that.") Or predators may even claim that they acted only from the highest motives. ("I only did it so that I could get in good with Ramon and then help get you that promotion you want.") Worse yet, villagers know that some predators actually believe these rationalizations. So a victim will never get the satisfaction of a clear-cut admission, "Yes, I set you up."

Villager vulnerabilities: the threat of being abandoned

In addition to the heightened sense of vulnerability that goes along with not wearing armor and with being such an easy quarry to predators in the village, villagers are also vulnerable to being hurt by being abandoned. Villagers feel that they need the acceptance and protection of the group in order to survive. To be deserted by other people and to be left to fend for themselves, then, feels deeply unsettling. To be thrown out of their group would be seen as a profoundly hostile act by a villager. Even being threatened with this would feel hostile.

Villagers experience appeals based on loyalty to the group they belong to as powerful pressure—even coercion. Such an appeal contains an implicit message that if the villager disappoints the group, he or she might be seen as

no longer being a "real" member any more. Since the "wrong" decision could be seen as having serious consequences, villagers can sometimes experience appeals to loyalty as threats.

Villager vulnerabilities: the drawbacks

Not surprisingly, the combination of no armor and heightened vulnerability has some important drawbacks.

First, villagers may take things too personally. That is, they may see every instance of warrior "pushing" as hostility. In the "village," it's easy to hurt people who are unprotected. When you combine this with the village taboo against direct conflict, villagers naturally conclude that any harm done to them is deliberate. Villagers assume that in an unarmed world where everything is centered around relationships, the only reason someone would act aggressively toward them is personal animosity. Hurts register deeply with villagers, and they often are remembered for a long time. Some villagers have been known to nurse grudges for years.

Villagers' considerable vulnerability and sensitivity to conflict may easily lead them to misinterpret and overact to aggression. In the villagers' world, engaging in direct, public conflict is tantamount to declaring war. Accordingly, we might say that while warriors regard aggressive competitors as *opponents*, villagers often see them as *enemies* who have declared themselves as such. For example, a villager might easily interpret a co-worker's criticism of a villager's suggestion at a meeting not only as a desire to impress the boss, but also as a personal attack designed to publicly humiliate the villager. As a result, when villagers react to someone else's aggression, they probably cross the line and respond with hostility more often than is called for.

Warriors and villagers: problems and solutions

From everything we've seen about the differences in how warriors and villagers express and perceive aggression, it should be apparent that there is plenty of room for misunderstanding. As a result, warriors and villagers alike make the workplace hostile and uncomfortable for each other without intending to and without realizing it.

1. *Villagers can misconstrue ordinary warrior competitiveness as a personal attack.* Because business is essentially a competitive enterprise, misunderstandings are particularly likely on this score.

Warriors can help the situation by keeping conflicts professional. In short, don't "stab" villagers. Constantly shooting down a villager's ideas, mocking a villager's contribution at a meeting or hurling insults ("That's one of the stupidest ideas I've ever heard") doesn't help. Other warriors may take such comments as a harmless challenge that they readily respond to, but villagers might read it as a declaration of war and start planning guerrilla retaliation. Accordingly, warriors should not make the mistake of thinking that a villager who apparently "folds" in such a situation and fails to fight for his or her idea is either weak or unaggressive.

In the same spirit, warriors should appreciate the emotional connection that villagers feel to their part of the business. So if you're engaged in "turf wars," a merger, reorganization, consolidation, expansion, or downsizing, try to handle the inevitable difficulties and hard feelings in a way that villagers can see that you're sensitive to the human impact of the process.

At the same time, villagers have to interpret such behavior as just part of a game that warriors play from 9 to 5. It really is the case that "it's just business." Don't take it personally. Warrior aggressiveness doesn't spring from personal malice. Having an outwardly aggressive, even abrasive, style does not make a warrior an evil person against whom a war should now be waged.

Recognize, however, that some warriors will pay attention only to someone who "stabs" back. And in such a situation a villager's best strategy may be to learn how to wield a sword. This may mean acting in a way that you're not comfortable with. You may have to adopt a much more direct, argumentative and combative style of communication than you're used to. You may have to make explicit demands or adopt a very hard line in negotiations. You might have to show anger. You may even have to engage in exchanging ritual (but not personal) insults. Remember, however, that this is only "war games," not the real thing. So be careful not to cross the line. And as long as you stay within accepted warrior traditions, your adversary won't take it personally.

2. *Even the playful, ritual banter or mutual insults that warriors engage in daily can feel like barbs to villagers.* Remember, villagers aren't wearing armor in these encounters. Moreover, neither male nor female villagers find "stabbing" at other people fun.

Again, warriors can ask themselves if any business purpose is served by such exchanges with villagers. If you're a manager, you might try to quietly derail this practice for the sake of group cohésion. Mutual "ribbing" may let warriors bond, but it eventually alienates villagers. Even villagers who can "fence" with warriors can find it forced and tedious, and they resent being pressured to do something that's not natural for them. And warriors should not misread a villager's reaction or refusal to join in. It's not that villagers lack a sense of humor. It's just that given their psychology, the traditions of the village, and their overriding concern with group harmony, they prefer humor that doesn't risk hurting someone's feelings.

How should villagers who are uncomfortable with this practice handle the situation? Above all, don't take things too seriously. If you work with warriors who enjoy "busting" one another before getting down to business, just quietly wait them out. Don't feel that you have to join in. Your career will not stand or fall on your ability to engage in verbal jousting. However, if your colleagues are engaged in more than the usual harmless sparring—for example, if their comments are racist, sexist or in some other way offensive—either leave and come back in a few minutes, or, particularly if you're a manager, make it plain that you consider this kind of humor unacceptable and unprofessional. (There is no doubt a company policy proscribing it.)

If you become a target of good-natured joking, first try not to read it as personal hostility. In fact, it might be a compliment. Some warriors "bust" only people they like. In any event, if it makes you uncomfortable, the best strategy is simply to try to put on some "armor." Remember that the point of the banter is to prick you into reacting. So, again, wait it out. If you won't "play," you'll be seen as an uninteresting opponent, and you'll ultimately be left alone. Another strategy would be to try to change the tone of the encounter. Opt for clever, silly or even self-deprecating humor.

Don't respond in a way that will be read as if you're "losing" in the exchange. For example, if you get angry, you'll be seen as overreacting. If you get nasty, you'll be seen as being indefensibly hostile—violating the warrior code by using "real bullets" when the assumption was that everyone would use "blanks."

If you become the target of intentionally hurtful remarks, the worst thing you can do is to try to put an end to them by publicly "nuking" your opponent with a particularly cutting remark. This will instead be taken as a challenge, and you'll guarantee that the contest will continue.

3. *Warriors can experience villager attempts to avoid conflict as hostility.* Villagers will avoid telling other people bad news if it might get them angry and lead to a fight. Warriors, however, feel that this is deceptive, manipulative and threatening.

Villagers abide by the village taboo against outward conflict so much that they will frequently wait until the last possible moment to tell someone something that could make him or her angry. Villagers especially avoid saying that something might go wrong because they feel that there's no reason to say anything until the bad news is definite. Villagers do this in order to keep the peace and to avoid a fight, but warriors take this as a hostile act.

First, warriors like to be in control of things that affect them. If warriors are going to face a problem, they want as much time as they can get to plan how to handle it. Villagers often compound a

situation because their delay lets a problem gets worse. They will sometimes even conceal problems past the point where they can be fixed. This infuriates warriors because they feel that by avoiding the risk of angry words, villagers deny them the chance to protect themselves. This makes warriors feel that villagers are undependable cowards, who only make their world more dangerous.

Second, concealing information from a warrior triggers the feeling that the warrior is being controlled, deceived, and manipulated. The only reason that warriors conceal information from one another is to use it as a weapon. So warriors assume that this must be behind a villager's concealment. As we have pointed out earlier, the fear of being controlled is a major vulnerability for warriors.

How can this difficulty be handled? First, warriors must make it easy for villagers to give them bad news. Villagers balk because they want to avoid conflict so badly. If warriors react angrily or abusively to a villager's bad news, they're teaching the villager to avoid, dissemble or even lie to them. So it would help for warriors to keep as calm as possible in front of a villager at times like these. (Then go outside and blow up.)

For their part, villagers must first see the real-life consequences of their actions. Their intention to keep the peace will usually backfire because their attempt to avoid a conflict actually makes it worse. When warriors ultimately discover the truth, they will be 10 times more angry with villagers who "manage bad news" than they would have been if they were told about the possibility of a problem at the outset. Indeed, at that point, because warriors now feel threatened with being controlled, they're actually more angry about feeling that a villager manipulated them than about the original problem.

Villagers must accept that the results of their behavior are more important than their intentions. They must respect a warrior's desire to know all the news—good, bad, definite, possible—that can affect a warrior's life. They must learn how to handle conflict and warrior anger. And, above all, their commitment to full and candid communication must become stronger than their desire to avoid a fight.

4. *Some villager attempts to "connect" can feel intrusive to warriors.* For example, being touched during a conversation or being pressured to talk about a problem can feel intrusive and smothering—a violation of a warrior's sense of privacy.

Villagers need to remember and respect the fundamental difference between themselves and warriors—warriors don't experience closeness the same way that villagers do. If you're a villager, be sure to see this as analogous to your experience of competition. While you become uncomfortable at the very thought of conflict, many

warriors can't get enough of it. (That's why warriors—male and female—can untiringly watch one sports contest after another.) And while you probably can't get enough of having deep, personal conversations with friends, warriors can quickly get to the point where this feels like too much of a good thing. Closeness may always feel welcome to villagers, but it's problematic for warriors. Too much closeness compromises a warrior's sense of independence and can trigger a warrior's sense of danger. Don't invade a warrior's space—either physically or emotionally.

This is easier said than done, however, because warriors often engage in lots of physical contact with each other. They'll slap one another on the back, grab an arm, or jab one another in the side. And this may make villagers feel that warriors are comfortable with all sorts of touching. But warrior touching is actually impersonal. It's more aggressive than intimate. In fact, one of the reasons that warriors get uncomfortable with villager touching is because of its intimacy. Friendly touching is often misread by warriors as a sexual come-on. And this feels especially intrusive on the job.

It's also important for villagers to respect the fact that if warriors are upset about something, they may not want to talk about it. Respect a warrior's need for silence and solitude. Do not try to pressure warriors into talking when they don't want to. At times like this, warriors aren't just sulking in their caves. They're thinking about how to handle the problem. If you're a villager, you'll find it difficult not to pressure a warrior on your project team or your warrior boss to open up. You want to know what's going on, you want to help and, because the matter affects you, you feel that you're entitled to know. However, pushing warriors to talk will be experienced by them as an insensitive and aggressive intrusion.

How can warriors help handle these situations? First, at least by remembering how important it is for villagers to feel connected, you may see villagers' actions as less irritating. And you might feel comfortable taking the initiative at establishing a connection with them in a way that takes care of both your needs.

For example, before getting down to business, you might engage in some small talk in which you prompt villagers to talk about themselves: "How are things in the field this month?" "What do you think of that new product?" "How are you and your co-workers affected by the merger?" Even, "Are you fully recovered from the flu?" The key here is to show that you listen to the answer. Make eye contact. Nod your head. Say: "hmmm," "I see," "I understand," "I'm sorry to hear that," "I know what you mean." All of us feel a connection with and become well-disposed toward people who act interested in what we say. Resist the temptation to contribute anything of your own until the villager has talked for a while. Then add a little something from your point of view and get on with things.

If you're confronted by a "touching" villager who can't read the more subtle signs that you're uncomfortable, you might make a joke about your "personal space."

If you have a problem that you want to be left alone with, be aware that if you just clam up, the villagers around you will start getting nervous. They'll feel disconnected from you, and they'll also assume that you're probably upset at them. Accordingly, take the initiative at keeping the connection and giving reassurance. Say something like, "I'm upset about something, but it's not you. I'll tell you about it when I feel ready to talk, but first I need to think through it on my own. Thanks for being patient."

5. Villagers must respect the fact that warriors feel attacked by villager aggression and that they see it as underhanded.

Warriors are offended by how villagers fight. Villager aggression violates a deeply held warrior code that any contest should follow accepted rules of combat. For example, warriors are incensed that a villager would try to use a warrior's own friends against him or her.

Warriors see it as hypocritical that villagers complain that warriors are aggressive while pretending that they themselves aren't. Although these villagers believe this about themselves, warriors take these denials as either insincere posturing or a sign of stupidity. Warriors are particularly offended when villagers personalize a dispute and respond to warrior competitiveness with hostility. Warriors see this as being mean-spirited—something that is especially two-faced in light of the image villagers project.

Villagers, then, must accept the consequences of their aggression. Covert, indirect aggression makes the workplace as offensive for warriors as open, abrasive conflict does for villagers. The fact that dealings with an adversary are kept outwardly friendly makes the environment, if anything, even more hostile to warriors than if the situation were more honest. Villagers must not be surprised when warriors answer aggression with aggression. Villagers who genuinely want a cooperative, harmonious work environment must learn how to resolve differences through direct communication and negotiation. Villagers must give up "guerrilla warfare."

For their part, warriors have to accept that villagers fight differently. Villagers are not cowardly and deceitful because they're guerrillas. This is simply their natural style. It's not that they have no code in how they fight; they have a different code from warriors. And the village taboo against open conflict is so strong that many villagers have trouble seeing guerrilla warfare as genuine aggression.

Accordingly, when warriors are the victims of villager aggression, they must make it plain in terms that villagers can relate to that this is what's going on. Warriors must call villagers

on their aggression and be explicit about why they find it offensive. For example, "I understand from other people that you didn't like the way I reacted to your idea at last week's meeting. I'll be happy to talk to you, so that we can resolve this. I want you to know, however, that I'm disappointed that you didn't talk to me directly. When you go behind my back, it makes me feel that you don't trust me. It also makes me wonder whether there are other ways that you aren't open and honest with me. And all of this is weakening our working relationship."

Our opening dilemmas

Let's return to where we started in this chapter, see if we can make sense of the opening vignettes, and figure out how to defuse these situations: Bill's "stabbing" Vicki, Gloria's undermining Jarod, Helen's smothering Corinne, and Cindy and Anne feeling hostile toward Vicki. It should be apparent that, at each turn, these problems arise from differences in how people "push" or in what makes them feel pushed.

Vicki and Bill: stabbing

We started with Bill giving Vicki a hard time about her being the quarter's top performer. Bill is obviously a warrior; Vicki, a villager. Vicki's understandably annoyed because she takes Bill's comments to be aggression. She feels "stabbed." But she's reading more into Bill's remarks than is there. Bill is very competitive, and it's no surprise that he'd be unhappy with losing. But his taunts are more of a challenge—possibly even a sign of respect—than a petty and mean-spirited display of sour grapes. Bill wears "armor," and he and other warriors probably "stab" at each other all the time. For Bill, this is normal, competitive behavior.

Vicki's best bet is probably to follow Jarod's advice: not to let it bother her. She should just smile and say, "In your face, Bill!" Of course, Vicki always has the option of speaking to Bill privately, telling him that what he does makes her uncomfortable, and asking him not to do it any more. But whether this is a good idea will depend on her relationship with Bill (being friends makes it easier), just how pronounced a warrior he is (some warriors might take her request to be a sign of weakness), and what the company's culture is like (if gibes are the norm, Vicki's complaint will likely go unheard and seem odd; if Bill is out of line with what usually goes on, Vicki is doing him a favor by bringing it up). Vicki has to decide which option will make it easiest for her to no longer feel "stabbed" in such situations.

If Bill notices that Vicki doesn't "stab" back and that she either ignores or is annoyed by his comments, the sensible thing for him to do is to back off—now and in the future. He can always talk to Vicki about it, if he wants to. But Bill has nothing to gain by continuing to "ride" her and to risk

that a co-worker may start thinking to herself that Bill is just an aggressive jerk.

In this situation, it makes the most sense for Bill to change his behavior. It's easier for warriors to resist stabbing villagers than it is for villagers to develop a thicker skin. More importantly, "stabbing" in this case doesn't help anyone do a better job. In fact, it's just the opposite. Vicki doesn't feel spurred on by Bill's challenge; she's mad at him. And this doesn't add anything to Bill's output. There's no way that what's going on makes anyone more productive.

Vicki and Bill: arguing

Vicki also complains that Bill attacks her every word. Vicki is simply encountering ordinary warrior argumentativeness, but she experiences it as an almost personal assault. Vicki associates Bill's arguing with his "riding" her about her success, so it's somewhat understandable that she'd take it personally.

Seen in that light, Bill should realize that not everyone is comfortable or adept at arguing. Warriors like Bill enjoy arguing. They rise to a challenge, generally refining and improving their ideas in response to someone's criticism. Many villagers, on the other hand, prefer to test out their ideas in a less confrontational manner. They first want to hear what's good about their ideas so that they can see if there's something there to build on. They are happy to hear other people's suggestions and revisions, and they enjoy the group process of putting something together. Accordingly, they're most comfortable testing ideas in a harmonious setting, and they consider arguing to be bad form.

Obviously, warriors like Bill can take pains to make it clear that they see arguing against someone's position at a meeting as part of the way they do their job—it's nothing personal. And they can try to be more open to a different way of testing ideas. At the same time, however, villagers like Vicki should be sensitive to the fact that this is generally a very positive use of warrior aggressiveness. Warriors aren't "mixing it up" for fun in those occasions. They're trying to do a good job. And if they give this up, their performance will probably flag. So a strong business argument can be made for not asking Bill to change his style.

Perhaps the best way to handle this matter is to orchestrate a meeting so that both styles—collaborative and argumentative—surface at a meeting in their own turn. In that way, both villagers and warriors alike will feel that they've had a chance to work in a way they're most comfortable. And the organization will get the benefits of the different contributions that each can make.

Jarod and Gloria: sabotaging

Gloria is a villager using guerrilla tactics against Jarod. She obviously took his lack of assistance personally, was hurt by it, and is now responding in kind. Characteristically for a villager, her aggression is denied and indirect—but effective. She gets Jarod angry and makes his job difficult. And all the while, she's outwardly civil toward him and claims that nothing's wrong.

There's a good chance that, like Vicki, Gloria has misread the situation. As far as we can tell, there's been no explicit communication between Jarod and Gloria about why he didn't back her request. Or if he did offer an explanation, Gloria obviously didn't find it believable or satisfying. Given this, a villager like Gloria would most likely assume that Jarod refused because he thought there was something wrong with her. And that's why she's hurt. Of course, there are many other possible reasons for Jarod's action. But that's how villagers see things. Accordingly, if Jarod's refusal didn't stem from some problem about Gloria herself, he should have taken pains to make sure that Gloria knew this. (And if the problem was with Gloria, common courtesy should have led Jarod to explain this to her in a way that was sensitive to her feelings.)

However, Gloria is equally responsible for not having clarified the situation before things got out of hand. Gloria clearly should know why Jarod acted as he did before she declares war on him. And no matter what Jarod's reason, she should ask herself whether deciding that Jarod is now the "enemy" and going to war against him is the best path to take. Blaming him and settling a score is sure to sour Jarod's relationship with her. Even though Gloria's campaign is clandestine, Jarod is aware of what she's doing. Gloria's guerrilla warfare is sure to backfire eventually.

Jarod, however, probably thinks that since he's talked to Gloria, the current problem is all her fault. And Jarod has tried to talk to her—but not hard enough. In fact, Jarod is part of his own problem. He has accepted Gloria's "everything's fine," when her actions say the opposite. And Gloria probably takes this as Jarod's way of saying that he realizes that she's justified in what she's doing. Jarod has only one realistic option. He must make it plain to Gloria that despite the pretense, he recognizes her guerrilla campaign for what it is, he's upset about it, and he wants to make peace. Until he does that, Gloria has no small amount of influence over an important part of his life.

Helen and Corinne: smothering

Helen is a villager who feels connected to the people she likes by physically touching them. Corinne is a warrior who prefers physical distance. Helen is no doubt trying to be friendly to Corinne, but her touching feels aggressive and intrusive instead. Corinne is feeling uncomfortable, and she's frustrated because she doesn't know what to do. As a result, she's getting annoyed at everyone around her.

Corinne's initial strategy of diplomatically trying to move to a different chair was a good idea for the immediate situation. If it had worked, Corinne would have felt more comfortable, and Helen's feelings would have been respected. However, even if it had worked, it would only have been a patch job for the moment. Until Corinne says something, Helen's probably going to assume that, like herself, Corinne likes the small, friendly touches.

Earlier in this chapter, we suggested a joking strategy for this kind of problem. A more direct approach, of course, is for her to say something like, "Helen, I know that touching me when we talk is your way of being friendly, and I genuinely appreciate the gesture. However, you and I are very different on this score, because being touched makes me uncomfortable. That's why I don't touch you back, which I feel badly about, because I'm sure it disappoints you. However, that's just the way I am. It means a lot to me that I can tell you this because I want to feel that whenever we meet on the job, we both feel comfortable. I feel good about the fact that I can count on you to respect my need for space from now on."

The average villager will readily respond to such remarks. Helen would see Corinne as sharing something personal, and this would make her feel connected to Corinne. The request that Helen not touch Corinne would, thus, not make her feel that Corinne was pushing her away.

At the same time, villagers like Helen must be sensitive to the fact that warriors like Corinne simply need greater amounts of space. The fact that Helen is simply trying to be friendly is, unfortunately, irrelevant. She clearly did not pick up on Corinne's discomfort. She has to be more perceptive of and sympathetic to warrior sensitivities.

Vicki, Cindy and Anne: threatening

At the end of the meeting Vicki was cornered by Cindy and Anne. The exchange made Vicki feel guilty and disloyal for not sticking together on what her friends regarded as a "woman's issue."

Vicki is upset for a variety of reasons. First, Cindy and Anne essentially accuse Vicki of being a "bad villager" by not supporting the day-care proposal. Vicki's friends charge her with disloyalty and, by implication, putting her own interest ahead of the group. Villagers are deeply hurt by accusations of disloyalty—whether they're leveled by villagers or warriors. More importantly, however, Vicki is upset because she's being threatened. One of a villager's great vulnerabilities is a fear of abandonment—being thrown out of the "village" and being left alone. In essence, Cindy and Anne presented Vicki with a serious warning and a threat. This is definitely a case of villager hostility.

Notice that Cindy and Anne take Vicki's action personally—something that villagers have an unfortunate tendency to do. Vicki is just trying to do her job, but her friends inject their friendship into the mix. The friendship, of course, is important to Vicki. And that's why she's so upset.

Because Cindy and Anne are also villagers, Vicki's best tactic for making peace with them is to get them to see the bigger "village" involved. Vicki identifies with all of the women in the company, but she also feels responsible for looking out for the well-being of other people in the firm. And her expertise as an accountant makes her feel that establishing a day-care center would put the welfare of other people at risk. If Vicki can get Cindy and Anne to appreciate the strength of her feelings, and if she can get them to see that she feels torn between her duties to two different, but overlapping villages, her friends' anger should at least abate a little.

Had Vicki thought about the matter ahead of time, she might have spoken to her friends privately, explained her position, and tried to reach some accommodation with them. Without advance warning, they probably felt "blindsided" by Vicki. And that surely accounts for some of the intensity of their reaction.

For their part, Cindy and Anne must first ask if they read Vicki's action correctly. They apparently viewed Vicki's comments at the meeting as a hostile act against their "village." And absent any advance warning, it's understandable why they might. Nonetheless, they should ask themselves if they might be overreacting to the situation. And they should save the heavy artillery until they've had a chance to talk to Vicki under better circumstances. The two women must also appreciate the seriousness of their response to Vicki. They may be upset, but they must ask themselves if threatening another villager with abandonment is appropriate in this situation.

Giving one another a hard time on the job

In various ways, warriors' and villagers' differing sensibilities about aggression make trouble in the workplace. Largely without intending it, warriors and villagers harass one another through actions and comments that feel hostile on the receiving end. Warriors stab, while villagers sabotage, undermine and smother—at meetings, at the water cooler, at lunch, on the phone, in memos, to one another's face and behind each others' backs. And once we've crossed the line with one another, our jobs are affected. We avoid dealing with the people who make us uneasy. We start using a new entrance to avoid going past their desks. We stop going to the company cafeteria in the hope of avoiding them. When we go to work, we feel like we're entering enemy territory. And there's no way that anyone can do their best when they feel that way about their jobs.

It's important both to ride herd on how we ourselves "push" in the workplace and to be conscious of how our co-workers do so. We have to be sensitive to the fact that what's normal for us may feel hurtful to a colleague. And, at the same time, we have to realize that someone's shot at us may not be intentional at all. The more that we can keep in mind that warriors and villagers assert themselves very differently and also have dramatically different vulnerabilities, the more likely we can get through the day without stepping on one another's toes.

Chapter Five

Sexual harassment

Men and Women at Work

As Basaam went to sit down to wait for his flight to be called, he spotted Judy, a former co-worker, on the other side of the lounge. He headed her way looking forward to a pleasant reunion. But as he got close, he realized that Judy was just glaring out the window, and he got the feeling that she was angry.

"Excuse me, sweetcheeks, but you're in my seat," he said, causing Judy to throw her best "drop dead" look his way. "So am I supposed to turn to stone now or are you going to ask me to join you?"

"You pig. You guys are all alike," she spat out. "I'm sorry, Basaam, it's good to see you. But it's been a bad day," she observed.

"Hey, I never would have guessed," Basaam replied. "So do we play 20 questions, or do you save me the trouble and just tell me what's with the 'men-are-swine' attitude?"

"I don't think I can stand one more day in this job. Wholesale food is just such a macho industry that it's making me crazy," Judy explained.

"Yeah, so what else is new? You knew that going in," observed Basaam.

"I know," said Judy, "and I thought I could handle it. I knew that lots of the guys would think that I didn't belong in the field. I knew some people would think that the only reason I got this job was that corporate wanted to increase the number of women in that part of the business. I also knew that some of the guys see foul language and locker room humor as part of what any woman has to accept if she wants this kind of job. And most of the time, I can handle whatever comes along. I don't think the guys deliberately try to offend me. Sometimes they're thoughtless about what they say, but normally it doesn't get to me."

"So what happened today?" asked Basaam.

"Two things," sighed Judy. "The first was at a meeting on whether we could persuade supermarket chains to take on a new product. The problem was in what my district manager said in trying to describe what a tough sell this was going to be: 'Squeezing something new onto those shelves is going to be rough because they're so full already. Those shelves are tighter than a virgin.' I couldn't believe he said that!"

"Come on," remarked Basaam, "lots of guys talk that way. He didn't say what he did to get you upset. You're blowing this way out of proportion."

"I don't care if I am," said Judy, getting angry again. "I'm furious that he'd say something like that."

"You said there were two things," observed Basaam, trying to change the subject. "What was the other?"

"I had lunch with Harold," Judy answered, "and he was criticizing the company's new sexual harassment guidelines. He said that he thought it was stupid to think that a little joking and flirting would get in the way of a woman doing her job."

"That's the big deal? Frankly, I agree with him," Basaam noted curtly.

"Give me a break!" said Judy, impatiently. "I wouldn't be so upset if that's all that happened. I told Harold about the time Tony reached under the table and grabbed my knee when we were interviewing a potential new broker. It broke my concentration and put me on edge for the rest of the interview. I'm sure that Tony did it to make me look bad to the customer.

"But Harold thought that was just the greatest thing. He said, 'Grabbing you under the table at a meeting? What a great move! I'll have to remember that next Wednesday.' I told him that if he did anything like that I'd punch him in the nose right in the middle of the meeting. But he just laughed and said: 'If you make a scene, you'll look like an idiot. I'll say it was an accident, and you'll come off as being so uptight, that you cry 'harassment' every time some guy bumps into you. It'll be fun. I'll save you the chair beside me.' I'm furious that he'd threaten me like that."

"Threaten you?" replied Basaam unsympathetically. "Aren't you going off the deep end? Do you really think that Harold would grab you at a meeting? Besides, even if he did, everybody knows that he's a jerk. I thought you had real problems. What is this, PMS?"

"Boy, you've been a big help," said Judy sarcastically. "You used to be a nice guy. What's wrong with you?"

"Wrong with me? Nothing. I'm fed up with all of this stuff about how men are scum. Women do their share, only they get away with it," Basaam replied angrily. "I know. It happened to me."

"Sure it did," mocked Judy. "You expect me to believe that some sweet young thing harassed big, strong you? Give me a break."

"That's just how everyone reacted. No one would believe me. That's why I left the company. You remember Phyllis, the one who'd flirt with anything in pants? Well, she decided that she had the hots for me and came on with both barrels. I asked her to cut it out, but she thought it was fun. I even switched to using the south entrance just to avoid walking past her office every morning. Well, one day she got wise to what I was doing and met me there. As I walked in, Phyllis struck this sexy pose, stuck out her chest and purred, 'Say Basaam, do you like my new dress?' Frank, my boss, was 10 steps behind and saw the whole thing.

"Later that day I told Frank what Phyllis was up to, but I could tell he thought either that I was ridiculous for making an issue of it or that I spent my days on the job prowling for women. Then in my next review, he said that my numbers weren't as high as they should be, and then he said something vague about my not being management material. I've never been so humiliated. I'm sure that being kept out of management was connected to the way Frank saw the episode with Phyllis. And there was no way I could stay after that."

"I always wondered why you left so quickly," mused Judy. "So I guess we both got shafted."

Sexual harassment

In the last chapter, we looked at some fairly common ways that warriors and villagers give one another a hard time. And by and large, once we take the time to look at how we deal with each other, we have a relatively easy time recognizing how other people may feel pushed around by us. However, there is no more controversial issue than sexual harassment. Because of dramatically different viewpoints among people, there is probably no topic that people disagree more about on the job. And because of the large amounts of money this is now costing companies, there is probably no problem that businesses want to avoid more.

In this chapter, we'll explain why people see this particular form of giving co-workers a hard time so differently,

we'll discuss the fact that both women and men get sexually harassed, we'll suggest how to handle harassing situations, and we'll return to Basaam and Judy. This chapter should help you prevent harassing situations from developing in the first place. It will make it easier for you to distinguish between unintentional harassment and the real article. And that will make it easier for you to decide on the best course of action if you're faced with an uncomfortable situation on the job.

Sexual harassment and gender

In order to discuss the sensibilities involved in sexual harassment, however, we're going to have to shift the focus of our discussion toward gender and away from character type. The disagreement over what should count as sexual harassment is mainly between *men* and *women*, not between *warriors* and *villagers*. Nonetheless, what we said in the last chapter about differences in how warriors and villagers can feel hurt is directly applicable here. In the same way that warriors and villagers live in "different worlds" and have different sensibilities about being the object of someone else's aggression, most women have more reason to feel threatened by certain situations than most men do. At the same time, however, there are differences in the "worlds" of men and women that lead to men—warriors and villagers alike—experiencing their share of a slightly different form of harassment by women.

Sexual harassment defined

Just what is sexual harassment? In this chapter, we're going to use a simple, yet broad, understanding of the notion derived from the legal definition of the federal government's Equal Employment Opportunity Commission. For our purposes, sexual harassment is defined as follows:

Any unwelcome verbal or physical conduct of a sexual nature that— intentionally or unintentionally—seriously interferes with someone's performance on the job, makes them feel threatened or intimidated, makes them feel that they're the target of someone else's aggression or hostility, or makes their working environment feel offensive and very uncomfortable.

Note how wide a net we've cast. "Sexual harassment" includes any conduct of a sexual nature that can be offensive. It also includes things that people do or say with absolutely no intention of making someone else uncomfortable.

What kinds of male sexual conduct can be offensive to women in the office? What female sexual conduct can unwittingly come across as hostility on the job? These are the questions we must answer. (To keep this chapter a manageable size, we're going to limit our discussion to heterosexual harassment: men harassing women, women harassing men. Much of what we're saying, however, will obviously apply in situations where men sexually harass men and women sexually harass women.)

Deliberate sexual harassment and power

Harassment—sexual or otherwise— is about power. Deliberate harassment is about other people showing that they wield power over you: the power to make you do things you don't want to do; the power to make you put up with a situation that you find offensive; the power to make you feel demeaned, insulted, intimidated or even threatened. Harassment is about someone showing that he or she can be a hostile presence in your life and that there's nothing you can do to stop it.

When the harassment is sexual, antagonists hide their hostility behind the cloak of human sexuality. (Sadly, in pathological cases, they hide their aggression even from themselves and believe they're genuinely interested in the other person.) They aggressively advertise their own sexuality and mark others as objects of their interest. Harassers then use sexual language or rituals to unsettle their targets and to attempt to dominate them. They sexualize an atmosphere unnecessarily and inappropriately. They relate to their targets strictly as objects of sexual desire. And, of course, they do all of this against the will of the person being harassed and in a way that's designed to offend him or her.

Unintentional sexual harassment and power

Unfortunately, as we saw in the last chapter, it is possible to feel pushed around by someone without that person intending this. This is as true for sexual harassment as for the nonsexual sort. Indeed, much of the debate about sexual harassment stems from the fact that there is so much *unintentional* sexual harassment. Both men and women say and do things that make the workplace very uncomfortable for members of the other sex without intending to and without noticing it.

Like deliberate harassment, however, unintentional sexual harassment is also about power. That is, both sexes inadvertently create situations where some expression of human sexuality in the workplace makes members of the

other sex feel hurt, offended, pushed around or threatened. Remarks meant to be friendly land like punches. One sex's normal behavior feels aggressive to the other. And, like the other varieties of unintentionally giving people a hard time, unintentional sexual harassment can be traced to a lack of awareness about people's vulnerabilities and their sensibilities about aggression.

Accordingly, clarity on these issues can reduce the incidence of accidental harassment and can thereby make it easier to identify and stop deliberate harassment.

Sexual harassment: two types

About the only thing regarding sexual harassment that men and women agree on is that there are two types: *quid pro quo* and *hostile environment* harassment. The former applies to situations where meeting someone's sexual demands is a condition of employment or advancement: "sleep with me or I'll cancel your promotion." In the latter, what's at issue is sexual behavior that gets in the way of someone doing his or her job, or makes the working environment very uncomfortable. This includes sexual jokes or comments, flirting, requests for a date, love letters, or the presence of pictures, posters, calendars or magazines that range from mildly suggestive to pornographic. (In some companies, the *Sports Illustrated* swimsuit issue is an annual point of contention.) This kind of harassment can even extend to retaliating against someone after being turned down for a date by starting rumors or telling lies about him or her. The vast majority of all the sexual harassment complaints allege a "hostile environment."

There is also virtually no disagreement about the seriousness of *quid pro quo* harassment. Everyone condemns it as abusive, coercive and unethical. There is, however, wide and sometimes bitter disagreement between men and women over whether what's involved in hostile-environment complaints should really be thought of as harassment. Indeed, the differences in men's and women's attitudes about what constitutes a hostile environment are legendary.

Sexual harassment of women

Women label an environment "intimidating, hostile or offensive" much more readily than men do. In one survey, for example, three times as many women as men thought that "elevator eyes" (eyeing a woman's body up and down) constitutes harassment. Similarly, men and women responded differently when asked what their reaction would be to advances from a co-worker. Two-thirds of the males said they would be flattered. Yet the same percentage of women said that they would be offended. Also, women claim to be harassed more frequently than men. Formal studies report that 50 percent to 80 percent of women have experienced harassment in the workplace. By contrast, only less than 20 percent of men report

having been harassed. Women, then, are much more likely than men to see themselves as victims of sexual harassment.

There are probably four major reasons why women will label an environment as "hostile" more quickly than men will.

- Women are more likely than men to be victims of sexual and domestic violence.

- There is a long history of discrimination against women based on the idea that they are inferior to men. Many men still believe that women do not belong in business.

- Women are regularly intruded upon by men.

- In deciding when a comment, joke or come-on is appropriate, women place more emphasis than men do on the context.

What's important to realize, however, is that the impact of these differences is so profound that, as in the case of warriors and villagers, men and women can be said to live in different worlds. And the differences in these worlds produce dramatically different sensibilities between men and women about when they're being sexually "pushed around" by a member of the other sex.

Women, sexual harassment and domestic violence

The first reason why women experience a situation as harassing more quickly than men do is that women in our society are more likely than men to be victims of sexual and domestic violence.

- Women are more likely than men to be sexually abused as children and raped as adults.

- 75 percent of women who are raped know their attackers.

- Domestic violence is the leading cause of injury to women—more than car crashes, muggings and rapes combined.

- One in four women is likely to be abused by her partner.

- More than twice as many women are killed by husbands or boyfriends as are murdered by strangers.

- These statistics hold across virtually all economic, ethnic and racial lines in our society.

The average woman knows these statistics. And this produces a dramatic difference in when men and women experience someone else's behavior as threatening. As Judges Robert R. Beezer and Lex Kozinski of the Ninth Circuit of the U.S. Court of Appeals have written, "Conduct that many men consider unobjectionable may offend many women... Because women are disproportionately victims of rape and sexual assault, women have a stronger incentive to be concerned with sexual behavior. Men, who are rarely victims of sexual assault, may view sexual conduct in a vacuum."

In essence, women in our society actually do live in a "different world" from the one men inhabit. Women live in a world where being assaulted by a man you know and thought you could trust is a realistic and prudent fear, not paranoia.

Accordingly, sexual compliments or expressions of interest, particularly when made on the job, are problematic for most women. The flirtation may be genuine, but it may also be the first move of an aggressor. And the more a man persists in the face of no encouragement on the woman's part, the more that women feel that the latter is the case.

Women, discrimination and domination

The second major reason men and women view *hostile environment* harassment differently is the average woman's awareness of the history of discrimination and domination of women by men. A constant theme through 4,000 years of recorded history is that women are inferior to men and can legitimately be owned or ordered around. Even American law, despite its more than 200-year-old commitment to freedom and equality, allowed formal, open discrimination against women in business until the Civil Rights legislation of the mid-1960s. For a long time, women were barred from business. Many men still believe that business is a "man's world." Sexual discrimination is still legal in many other countries. And, of course, the fact that it is illegal in the United States does not mean that it doesn't still happen.

Again, women and men live in different worlds. Women live in a world in which it is a new—and by no means universally accepted—idea that women are equal to men, that they need not be subordinate to men, and that they belong in the business world.

Like the facts about sexual and domestic violence, the history of male domination produces a different sense of vulnerability in women than in men. In the same way that even an accidental remark reminds African-Americans of the attitudes that undergird hatred or discrimination can cut deeply, many women are profoundly offended by comments that recall any aspect of male domination. For anyone with a memory of the reality of domination, such comments say, "Look out, 'the bad old days' are still here." For most men in our culture, the idea of "domination" kindles a fear of what *could* happen. But for most women, it triggers something much stronger—a *memory* of what *did happen* and what, in many ways, *continues to happen.* And this contributes to the different sensibilities between men and women about when something registers as offensive.

And keep in mind some of the ways men enforced their supremacy in the workplace: to mock women, to treat the very idea of their being in a "man's world" as hilarious, to be condescending and patronizing toward them, to dismiss them as "emotional," and to see women's main value as sexual. All of these are excellent strategies for letting women know that they will not be taken seriously, and for warning them to "know their place." That's why so many women are immediately offended by humorous put-downs, flirtation and sexual joking.

"Hey, baby!"

The third reason that women label a situation harassing sooner than men do comes from the fact that women are so frequently the unwanted objects of men's attention. Women get cat-calls as they pass construction sites; they are hooted at as men drive by them; they're honked at and waved to in their cars by male drivers; they are ogled by strangers; they are pinched, fondled and rubbed against in buses, subways and elevators by men they've never met; they hear comments about their breasts, behinds and legs; and it is not unknown for a policeman to pull over an attractive female driver simply to get her telephone number.

(It's important to distinguish these practices from genuine, friendly compliments that both men and women know might elicit a positive response from a woman. A man knows that after he's just yelled from a passing car, "Hey, chickee baby! Shake those maracas!," a woman is not going to say to herself, "Wow! What a fantastic guy!," and burst into a sprint down Main Street in the hope of meeting him when he has to stop at a traffic light. Accordingly, we're talking here about comments that are designed to unsettle, not entice, the average woman.)

Many women come to have a fairly thick skin about all of this. Even so, these practices remain unsolicited, unwelcome, unpleasant and intrusive behavior that is beyond a woman's control. Minimally, being treated as a sex object can feel annoying, insulting, frustrating, offensive or demeaning. At worst, any of these actions can feel hostile and menacing.

Because men usually do not experience anything like the "construction site" phenomenon, this once again points to a basic difference in the worlds the two sexes inhabit. In a woman's world, unwanted, offensive, sexually intrusive behavior that a woman is powerless to stop is common.

The importance of context

The final reason men and women have different sensibilities about when a workplace is sexually offensive comes from the weight that women place on where an action takes place. Particularly when it comes to sexual comments or flirtatious actions, many women feel strongly that what is appropriate and inappropriate depends on whether a situation is personal or professional. The same comment that was funny at a party becomes offensive on the job. Flirtation that was enjoyed on the beach is seen as presumptuous and insulting at work. The context is critical. And most women consider sexualizing the workplace unprofessional and inappropriate.

Most women seem to draw sharper boundaries than men do between the world of work and the world of sex. And they do this because they feel that if they blur the line, it will work against them. There's the obvious concern that if a woman advertises her sexuality on the job, men and women alike may label her a "tramp" and suggest that she's trying to use sex to get what she wants. Many women in business contend that if they're seen as sexual by the men they work with, they get taken less seriously, and their job becomes more difficult to do. Many women complain that if men start relating to them sexually, men *stop* relating to them professionally.

Men probably let work and sex overlap because there are few negative professional consequences from a man's being labeled a "stud." Accordingly, men probably have fewer reservations than women do about openly flirting with or dating a co-worker. And most men are probably more comfortable than most women are with the jokes, comments, teasing and general raunchiness that goes with a sexualized workplace.

(Curiously, in an earlier chapter, we described an opposite pattern—that emotionally, villagers tend to blur the personal and professional, while warriors keep them distinct. Villagers may take it personally if someone criticizes their work. Yet warriors who are friends may be fiercely competitive without this affecting their personal relationship.)

Warrior and villager vulnerabilities

The four differences between men and women that we've just been considering reflect the key fears and vulnerabilities that we saw in the last chapter when we discussed ways that warriors and villagers can feel threatened by one another. That is, women in our society live in a world that feels menacing to female warriors and villagers alike. At the same time, male warriors and villagers live in a world that feels less menacing. Accordingly, the combination of these four factors produces in the daily lives of most women a sense of caution, apprehension or even danger that is considerably greater than that felt by most men in our culture.

- The higher incidence of sexual violence against women triggers the warrior's fear of being attacked by an enemy. Similarly, knowing that women are regularly attacked by men close to them evokes the villager's dread of discovering that someone she trusts has deceived her and is in reality a "wolf in the flock" preparing to prey on her.

- The reality of discrimination against women, the idea of female inferiority and attempts to keep women out of business strongly evoke the warrior fear of being dominated. Anything that reminds female warriors that it is only recently that they've stood a chance on the "battlefield" is bound to make them even more vigilant against attack than they normally would be. At the same time, the history of male domination of women reminds female villagers of the worst consequence of their decision to ban weapons, armor and open conflict from the village— they are powerless against any aggressor. Women are realistic enough to know that, like the traditions of the village, a company's policies will not stop some men from trying to dominate women or sabotage their careers. Similarly, the laws of the land do not protect people from the harm of the initial assault of an attacker.

- The fact that women are intruded on so frequently by men makes female warriors feel that they should constantly be on guard. The repeated comments, looks, and the like make warrior women feel that they are always being "stabbed" by men. And female warriors may also get on edge from being tired of trying to figure out whether the stabbing is in fun or in earnest. Villager women, of course, are going to have an even stronger reaction to unwanted comments because they don't wear the psychological "armor" or carry the "weapons" that wa... or women do. Being intruded upon so easily by men is only a reminder of a female villager's vulnerability. When you don't carry a sword, being noticed by a potential aggressor can evoke considerable amounts of fear and anger.

• The difference in the weight men and women place on context also plagues female warriors and villagers alike. The fact that women worry more about context in deciding whether certain behavior is appropriate or inappropriate could make female warriors worry that a man may be operating according to different rules. This may mean, for example, that what the female warrior sees as neutral territory, a male warrior may regard as the middle of a battlefield. And this would increase a female warrior's fear and sense of danger. Similarly, the difference in the importance of context increases the anxiety of female villagers because dealing with a man would feel like dealing with someone who was unpredictable and undependable. It would feel like trying to interact comfortably with someone who does not respect the norms and traditions of the village—or, worse yet, someone who comes from a village with customs the villager cannot comprehend.

The point of this discussion is that the experience of being a woman in the workplace makes female warriors and villagers alike feel more vulnerable and threatened than male warriors and villagers do. In their dealings with the opposite sex, men are less likely than women to be raped, beaten by someone they love, thought to be inferior because of their gender, hit on, or pinched by strangers. As a result, men's dealings with women in our society arouses less fear than women's dealings with men. Male warriors feel that their female enemies aren't quite as threatening. Male villagers experience their villages as safer.

The male equivalent: "Nice watch"

In understanding why men and women view sexual harassment differently, it is critical for men to appreciate just how different a woman's experience of the world is from a man's. The analogous situation for a man would be something like this:

Imagine that you're the kind of person who is uncomfortable in cities. However, for some reason or other—personal or professional—you now find yourself having to go to Mugville, the city you like least. Mugville has a soaring crime rate, drug use is depressingly high, the air is polluted and the people are unfriendly. Just arriving there puts you on edge. In the course of your visit, you read one urban disaster story after another. You even stop listening to the morning news because it seems that the reporters talk only about the murders that happened throughout the night. You are definitely uneasy being there.

Then one night you make a wrong turn and find yourself in one of the worst parts of town. As you're trying to make your way to a different neighborhood, however, someone comes up to you and says, "Hey, mister, what time is it?" Without thinking, you look at your watch and say, "It's about 8:15"—at which point the questioner observes admiringly, "Say, that's a nice watch."

Now take a moment and think about your reaction to this situation. Are you flattered by the compliment? Do you sidle up to the stranger, push back your sleeve so that he can see your timepiece better, and say with pride: "Yeah, ain't it great? I love this baby. It's a Rolex!"? Not very likely.

Instead, you're probably terrified that you're in danger and worry that you're about to be robbed. You feel foolish at having fallen for a mugger's oldest trick for finding out if you had anything worth taking. And you're ashamed that you were so careless that you made a wrong turn in the first place.

It's possible, of course, that all that's happened is that some stranger has given you a genuine compliment! However, under the circumstances, it's very unlikely that that's going to be your first interpretation of the situation.

The point of this imaginary urban excursion is that Mugville represents the "world" women in our society inhabit. Women are regularly victimized, women know this and, as a result, many have become distrustful of men—particularly in the workplace. Many have become especially suspicious about unwanted attention from men. Even when presented with a genuine compliment, many women instinctively react defensively. A comment like "Nice legs!" can register like the "Nice watch" remark in our scenario. Because of the domestic and sexual violence that women regularly face in our society, and because of the long-term effects of male domination, many women automatically react with anger, annoyance or fear to anything that suggests that they might become the object of some man's aggression.

Men, however, do not live in Mugville. They may visit there every now and then, but they can usually go

119

home to a safer place. And that means that men and women have very different sensibilities and vulnerabilities when it comes to deciding whether they're in a threatening situation at work.

When does a women feel sexually harassed?

The fact that women have good reason to feel more threatened in daily life than men do, then, is the key to understanding why a woman on the job might experience a situation as hostile, menacing, and intimidating even when a man is trying to be friendly and flattering. What kinds of things might trigger these feelings in the average working woman? Here are some possibilities.

- Any sexual overture from a co-worker can make a woman feel uneasy because she knows there's the risk she's being set up. Like villagers, women are always on the lookout for the "wolf in the flock"—the predator from their own company who appears on the outside to be harmless, even attractive.

- Women can experience a co-worker's unwanted interest— frequent compliments, phone calls, lunch invitations, letters or presents—as a sign that they have a "stalker" on their hands.

- References to a woman's body or remarks about her sexual attractiveness can make women feel afraid, angry or denigrated. Comments like "nice legs" or "so where does that tan line stop?" can raise the same fears that an unwanted suitor does. In addition, being regarded sexually when a woman wants to be seen professionally can make her feel belittled and dismissed by the men making the comments. Remarks like, "Working with you will be really difficult for me because I'm going to have such a hard time keeping my mind on my work" or "Let's work in your office—it's more intimate," can make a woman feel that she's conversing with a "problem," not a co-worker. And because any of this can make a woman feel that she is unfairly being put in a position where it will make her job harder to do, many women will respond with frustration and anger.

- Condescending and patronizing remarks at work, and office humor that trades on disparaging stereotypes of women (like "blonde jokes") can feel demeaning. Any of this can make a woman at work feel that the men around her think that because she's "only a woman," they will, at best, tolerate her in a subordinate position. Given the ways that male domination was enforced in the past, such remarks and jokes can even feel like a veiled threat. They can be read as a shot across the bow, warning a woman to "know her place"...or else. And this will feel especially intimidating if the comments are made by a woman's boss or by someone with even more power in the organization.

- Ordinary warrior banter, locker room behavior, or jokes that have an aggressive "edge" to them can feel hostile to many women because they may wonder whether this is just a cover for sexual aggression. Particularly if the women involved are villagers, they will see no humor in such typical warrior behavior. So they will fill the void with their apprehension and may experience what's going on as hostility.

- Sexual banter, teasing, comments or jokes that have an aggressive "edge" to them, obscene cartoons or E-mail messages, or other kinds of pornographic humor can feel hostile to many women because, like villagers, these women do not wear "armor." Many women find such jokes disturbing because it feels like the "construction site" has moved inside to the office. These comments also recall the attitudes

of men who are genuinely hostile toward women and who believe that women are inferior to men and don't belong in business. Such humor can make women doubt that they are accepted as equals by male co-workers who make such comments. Such humor can also make women wonder whether their progress at a company will ultimately be blocked. In particular, it raises the question of whether the humor masks a hostility that will prevent women from being placed in charge of men.

- Being told not to take things so seriously and to be a "good sport" about sexual jokes, flirting, or whatever can feel threatening to many women. Women on the job know that a basic fact of life in business is that, whether you're a man or woman, your success depends on how well you work with others—and on how well other people are willing to work with you. If a woman is accepted by the men around her and seen as "one of the guys," she knows that her job will be easier to do. The men will work with her the same way they work with each other. She'll get help and cooperation when she needs it. Co-workers will give her the "inside scoop" if something is cooking. They'll warn her if trouble is brewing. She'll get invited to lunch with the people she works with, and she'll be admitted to the inner circle. On the other hand, if a woman is, for any reason, labeled an outsider, she'll be professionally hamstrung. Accordingly, if a woman is told that she's overreacting to sexual humor or flirting, and that she should be a "good sport" about things, it feels like she's being threatened. Such remarks register with women as, "Shut up or you'll be thrown out of the group." Of course, being ostracized from the group makes it much harder to be successful.

- Most women find remarks about their menstrual cycle highly offensive for a number of reasons. First, comments like, "Do you have PMS?," or "What's wrong with you? Is it that time of the month again?" serve to dismiss a woman's feelings about something: "We can ignore what she's saying, it's just the hormones talking." Women feel demeaned and belittled by this. Second, such comments invade a woman's privacy. And because people looking to push others around often presumptuously cross personal boundaries, these remarks can feel like part of an

attempt to dominate or humiliate. That is, they can feel quite threatening.

"What's the big deal?"

Even if men are willing to concede that women live in such a "different world" that they have good reason to be more sensitive to the possibility of threats to their personal safety than men are, a man might still think that women overreact when it comes to sexual harassment. Many men think that women simply make too much of a fuss about a "hostile environment." "After all," a man might say, "it's only words, jokes or looks. It's not rape. It's not an explicit threat. It's not an assault. Guys are just trying to have some fun. Women aren't really hurt by any of this. What's the big deal? Why can't they cut us some slack?"

The issue here, however, stems from one more difference in the "worlds" that men and women inhabit. Simply put, there are many more predators in a woman's world than in a man's world. The average man would be shocked to learn how many men who work beside him actually set out to intentionally harass or dominate women on the job. The harmless guy who just likes to kid or flirt with women doesn't realize how different he is from these hostile, predatory males because these predators conceal this side of themselves from the men around them. And the average male doesn't realize that these predators use exactly the same "innocent," "playful" comments that he does when they start to harass a woman. As a result, the genuinely harmless man doesn't realize that the comments that he intends to be taken as signs that he's a fun guy actually make many women look at him as a possible "creep."

Most women make a "big deal" about sexual harassment, then, because, in addition to being more sensitive to potentially threatening situations, much more genuine harassment goes on at work than the normal man realizes. As a result, many women have strong reactions to the average man's thoughtless or tasteless remarks not because she's oversensitive, but because she's afraid that he's not what he seems on the surface. From her viewpoint, making a "big deal" about harassment is the only way to uncover and stop the predators.

"Women aren't really hurt"

Women also make a "big deal" about sexual harassment because, even though they aren't hurt physically by harassment, they are hurt emotionally more than most men realize.

Of course, a victim's reaction to being harassed will vary depending on such factors as the severity of the harassment, the emotional history of the victim and the woman's personality. Let's assume, however, that we're talking about a situation where a man repeatedly makes sexual comments or jokes to a woman, despite the fact that

she's let him know that this makes her uncomfortable. In fact, he enjoys making her uncomfortable, and he's going to keep it up. In short, we have a clear-cut example of hostile environment harassment. Among average women in our society—that is, women with the sensibilities we described earlier in this chapter—it's fair to say that being the victim of such harassment would feel like a kind of emotional assault.

The emotional assault: feeling victimized

The essential emotional response of being the victim of any misfortune is feelings of vulnerability and powerlessness in the face of some superior force. Because sexual harassment is about power, not sex, its victims will, first of all, feel the emotions associated with victimization.

However, part of the victimization involved in sexual harassment is experiencing the unpredictability of the harasser. Because harassers are intent on showing victims that they have the upper hand in the situation, they typically are unpredictable. This lets them enjoy feeling powerful, but it keeps their victims off balance and in a constant state of apprehension.

In addition, victims of sexual harassment also experience a prolonged state of anxiety. Skilled predators know how to extend the pain of their victims. They know just how far they can go in a situation so as to assault a victim emotionally while minimizing their own risk of any serious repercussions—something sure to increase the victim's pain, anger and frustration. Even in the case of less cagey harassers who are caught and disciplined, the victim must still endure a period of harassment during which the offense is documented.

A woman being victimized in the workplace is, therefore, thrown into a roiling sea of emotions that at times can feel overwhelming: powerlessness in the face of the harasser, dread at what he might do, fear over how this might affect a woman's job, rage at the unfairness, frustration at being unable to make it stop, self-doubt over whether the victim was in some way responsible for the harassment, impatience with the pace of most formal procedures, and the humiliation and other wrenching feelings that flow from being denigrated, mocked as inferior or pushed around.

The emotional assault: the workplace feels worse

It is even possible that such an experience will forever change a woman's sense of the workplace. A woman will now see the office or plant as a much less comfortable place than before. In particular, a woman will no longer be able to see the workplace as somewhere that she can be safe from emotional assault. She carries the memories of the harassment and the knowledge that it could easily happen again. She now knows firsthand that this sort of thing doesn't happen just to other people.

Harassment on the job typically results in a woman's changing her behavior or normal patterns. She'll do anything she can to avoid the harasser. She'll park in a different lot, use a different entrance, avoid certain parts of the building, change the path she takes to the copier, change when she goes to lunch, stop eating in the company cafeteria, even avoid certain company events. None of these individually is a monumental matter. But collectively they make someone's job much harder to do, because they're constant reminders that the workplace is now a fundamentally uncomfortable place. Indeed, it's no news that some women find the situation so unpleasant that they feel they have to find a job elsewhere.

The emotional assault: a no-win scenario

Another piece of the emotional assault that victims of harassment feel is the anger and frustration associated with the fact that they now find themselves in a no-win situation. Most women feel that once an aggressive man starts showing them attention, they've been put in a position where there are only bad options from which to choose: hostility now or hostility later.

If a woman tolerates an aggressive man's attention in the hope that he'll eventually stop, the problem will escalate. Because the man takes the woman's acquiescence as a sign that she likes him, the man gets more aggressive. This eventually pushes the woman to a point where she has to ask the man to stop. But this now makes the man angry because he feels that he's been misled. The woman is tarred as a "tease," and the man may look for ways to get even.

However, if a woman immediately rebuffs an aggressive man's unwanted advances, he will be angry at the rejection and brand her "frigid" or a "prude." This is a hostile reaction on his part. In the most extreme—and doubtless pathological cases—rejected suitors have been known: to stalk a woman, to call her friends to pry into her private life, to slander her to her friends, and even to allege falsely to her colleagues that she is promiscuous in an attempt to ruin her reputation.

Many women see this no-win harassment scenario as akin to another one that they already face in the workplace. As one woman put it, "Men want women to look great—well-dressed, in good shape, sexy, perfumed, made-up. But when we actually look that way, men treat us sexually, not as professionals." Of course, women are not alone in facing such no-win scenarios. The women's harassment scenario is equivalent to what many men experienced as boys with the "schoolyard bully." If you resisted, he'd beat you up. If you gave in, he'd push you around even more. And men continue to encounter "schoolyard bullies" on the job in the competitor who decides you're his rival and won't leave you alone. He lords it over you when he beats you, and he's angry with you when he loses to you.

Is it about to happen to me?

Even so, our fun-loving, average guy might still object. "I agree," he concedes, "that women who are the victims of deliberate harassment are hurt. "But," he protests, "what most guys do doesn't fall into that category. Most guys are just trying to have some fun on the job—you know, loosen things up a little. And most women know that. They know that most of the guys who kid around aren't stalkers or predators. So I feel they're overreacting."

In a way, of course, this complaint is accurate. *Objectively*, most men at work are not threats to the women they kid around with. They are neither stalkers, predators nor woman-haters. So a fear-threat reaction on the part of a woman is an overreaction. However, because of everything we've been discussing in this chapter, women do not experience the world as a safe place *subjectively*. Virtually every working woman either has been harassed herself or knows a woman who has been. And that means that an "overreaction" is understandable. Women know the harm that comes from genuine harassment. And they are understandably sensitive to and even frightened by any event that makes them wonder, "Is it about to happen to me?"

What to do?

For all of the complexities involved in identifying when a situation may feel harassing to a woman, the answer to the question, "What should we all do in light of this information?" is quite simple.

- First of all, men must keep in mind the fact that women live in a more dangerous world than men do. Keeping in mind that women live in "Mugville" will make it easier for a man to judge whether something he's thinking of saying or doing will probably register as offensive to the women around him on the job.

- Men should get into the habit of asking women to explain their reactions. If a man does not understand a woman's reaction to something he's said or done, he should ask, "Did what I just do make you uncomfortable?" And if a woman answers, "Yes," it's critical for the man to ask, "Will you tell me why it made you uncomfortable?" This serves two purposes. First, it helps a man better understand the emotional impact of his actions on women. But it also helps a woman clarify and understand her reaction. It is not unusual for a woman to have difficulty articulating precisely why she finds a situation uncomfortable. And it will help both parties immeasurably if the details of the woman's reaction are spelled out.

- If you're a man, and a woman tells you that what you do or say makes her uncomfortable, don't try to make peace by sending flowers! You may think that sending flowers, candy, a gift or a card is a safe way of mending fences. But this is the worst thing you can do. Because these are also traditional romantic gifts, a woman's first feeling will be that you're continuing to harass her. And this will make her even more upset because she'll now conclude that the harassment was deliberate, not accidental. Just say that you're sorry, promise that you won't do it again, turn the page on the episode, and get back to work. Assume that anything else will backfire.

- If a woman encounters an uncomfortable situation, she must communicate this fact quickly and clearly to the men involved. Speaking up immediately is critical for two reasons. First, this is the only way to change an uncomfortable situation. Many women delay saying anything to a man be-cause they hope that the man will stop bothering them if they simply ignore him. Many women resist telling a man that he's offended them because they don't want to hurt his feelings or provoke his anger. Silence is always an ineffective strategy! If a woman tolerates a male co-worker's flirtations or sexual jokes, he will conclude that she likes it. So he will continue. If a woman tolerates the behavior of a sexually hostile man, he will conclude that he can dominate her. So he will continue.

Second, saying something to a man is the only way that a woman can determine whether he offended her accidentally or deliberately. If it was an accident, he'll apologize and change—or try to change—his behavior. Most men have absolutely no desire to make women uncomfortable. They know that this in no way advances their interests. If the offensive behavior continues, however, there is no question that a woman is the target of a sexually hostile man. And that means that the longer she waits before taking formal action against him, the worse her situation will become.

• To say that it's important for women to let men know when they are uncomfortable with men's actions, however, doesn't mean it's going to be easy. Each woman must find a comfortable way of talking to men about this difficult topic. Some hints:

1. Discuss the issue with the man privately, rather than publicly.

2. Describe your reaction without apologizing for it or without blaming the man: "When you told that joke today, it made me feel that you think women are supposed to be 'barefoot and pregnant.' If that's true, I feel uncomfortable working with you."

3. Focus on the behavior involved, not the person: "I was upset after I saw you yesterday. When you came up behind me at my desk, put your hand on my back and leaned over my shoulder to see what I was typing, I felt intruded upon by you."

4. If you are particularly uneasy talking about your own reactions to what a man did, say something like, "I know you want to make a good impression with people at this company, but someone could get the wrong idea about you from things you say and do." This lets everyone save face.

• When confronted with a situation that makes you uncomfortable, respond seriously and clearly. For example, when women are faced with unwelcomed flirtation from male co-workers, they may respond with nervous giggling. Men read giggling in women not as nervousness but as enjoyment. It may be a signal for him to continue his behavior.

Sexual harassment of men

We have spent the vast majority of this chapter talking about what makes women feel sexually harassed because women are far more likely than men to lodge sexual harassment complaints against men than vice versa.

Yet men are harassed by women in the workplace. It may happen less frequently. There may be differences in what makes a working environment "offensive, hostile and intimidating" for a man than for a woman. But men are no more comfortable being harassed than women are—and this is equally true for male warriors and male villagers.

As is the case with men, most women probably don't intend to make men uncomfortable by what they say or do. And most women often aren't even aware when they do so. Nonetheless, men regularly feel uncomfortable and threatened by women's sexual comments and actions—more often than most women realize.

The key to understanding when women experience a situation as harassing is recognizing the ways that a woman's "world" produces certain emotional vulnerabilities. Obviously, recognizing when men feel harassed requires a similar appreciation for the vulnerabilities produced by a man's "world."

Sexual harassment, of course, is ultimately about power. As we've seen, women begin to feel uncomfortable and threatened at work when men's actions make them worry about the power of a physical assailant, the power of a sexually aggressive man or the power of discrimination. Men, on the other hand, can feel intimidated at work because of ways that women's actions remind men of forces which can dominate them. There are four factors involved.

- Despite our culture's tradition of male supremacy, most men feel powerless in life.
- Men are constantly reminded of the power of women— especially their sexual power.
- Men are regularly the target of "male bashing" by women.
- A woman's attack against a man is taken less seriously than a man's attack against a woman.

Who's in charge here?

Men feel as powerless in life as women do. Despite our society's myth of male supremacy, the average man does not feel that he is the master of his fate. Whether it's objectively true or not, most men do not subjectively feel that being male brings them more advantages and opportunities in life than being female. And they sometimes believe that the reverse is true.

The average man experiences his life as being dominated by people or circumstances beyond his control. It sometimes feels like the "job description" of being a man consists of a depressing list of responsibilities and prohibitions—backbreaking, and made up by someone else, to boot. For example:

- Obey the person in charge. (No matter how high in an organization a man rises, he knows that he will always have a boss.)

- Be prepared to fight, kill people and die in wars that someone else makes.

- Be prepared to financially support a spouse and children—even if any of these individuals decide to stop loving you or to leave you. Do not reveal to anyone the anxiety or fear that this responsibility produces.

- Don't publicly express any feelings that could be construed as weakness, such as dependency or fear—even though this will shorten your life. Vent your feelings through anger—which will also shorten your life.

As a result, men are hypersensitive to situations where someone seems to be gaining an edge on them. It only reminds them about how powerless they already feel. Feelings of being dominated are obviously threatening to male warriors and villagers alike.

Woman power

In a man's "world," women have great power—especially sexual power (just look at advertising).

- A man learns early in his relationships with women that attractive women can readily date and marry men who are older, richer, more powerful and more accomplished than he is or than the women themselves are. And he does not feel that he has an equivalent option.

- As men experience life, women do the choosing. A man can approach a woman he is interested in, but she's the one to say "yes" or "no."

- Men feel that if a woman wants to, she can manipulate a man. It doesn't even have to be anything deliberate or pernicious on her part. A man simply wants to please an attractive woman in the hope that she will like him.

- The average man is terrified of a woman's emotions. Most men are afraid of a woman's anger and a woman's tears. In the same way that women fear the stereotype of the hostile, sexually aggressive male, men fear the stereotype of the hysterical, crazy female. (We might call this the "Fatal Attraction" syndrome.)

Men especially fear the power of what we might call a woman's "flirtatious friendship" with a male boss or co-workers. (This is a sexualized, but not necessarily sexual relationship that plays off of the sexual tension between people. There's teasing, playful banter and just a hint that it may be more than a game.) And men feel disadvantaged and intimidated by this power. Confronting any superior power unsettles male warriors. Seeing a woman manipulate a man makes a male villager fear that female villagers are untrustworthy. Male villagers also worry that women may use their relationships with male villagers to advance their own ends.

Male bashing: guilt by association

While women experience more violence at the hands of men, men experience more blame at the hands of women. Men often feel that they live in a verbal "free-fire zone" simply because they're male. Women regularly engage in "male bashing" in the company of men, tarring all men with the same brush.

The downside of any liberation movement is that when people who have been oppressed begin venting their anger, it's not always directed at the appropriate target. Many women will speak about how "men" have discriminated against women and benefited from this fact, as though it were true of every man. As a result, good and decent men who have neither discriminated against any woman nor received any obvious benefit from the misdeeds of others feel that they are unfairly lumped together with their predatory brethren. It is not uncommon for a man who is genuinely supportive and respectful of

women to find himself being made to feel guilty about being a man, feeling frustrated that a woman is unfairly critical or suspicious of him, or feeling angry that he is supposed to make restitution for the sins of others.

Male warriors experience male bashing as hostility. Male villagers take it as a violation of the village taboo against open conflict. In either case, it feels threatening.

A double standard: "Don't hit your sister"

The social acceptability of male bashing also points to a double standard about aggression between the sexes. Female comics who mock men are considered to be funny; male comics who mock women are seen as sexist. That is, men live in a world in which violence against men by women—verbal or otherwise—is not taken as seriously as violence by men against women.

There are strong social norms that put men in an inferior position to women in a conflict. Men are taught not to retaliate against female aggression: "Don't punch your sister!" "Gentlemen" don't hit "ladies." It's assumed that if a woman strikes a man, she was provoked and had good reason. If a man strikes a woman, however, he is seen—by women and men alike—as a "brute." Moreover, the unspoken assumption is that a woman cannot hurt a man, no matter how hard she punches him. Male violence against women is seen as much more dangerous. Men feel that this double standard gives women an enormous strategic advantage.

As a result, if a man complains of being harassed by a woman, he takes considerable risks. He may be laughed at or be mocked as a "wimp." He may immediately be disparaged or distrusted for taking aggressive action against a "helpless" woman.

It obviously intimidates a male warrior to encounter a situation in which he cannot fight back against an attacker. And a double standard about aggression between the sexes feels hostile to male villagers. It means that they cannot trust that someone will recognize when they are hurt and come to their aid.

When does a man feel sexually harassed?

Even though men worry less than women do about members of the opposite sex physically intimidating them or dismissing them as irrelevant in the workplace, they are still vulnerable to feeling that they are the targets of a woman's aggression. Given what we've just seen about the primary ways that men are vulnerable to feeling that their environment is hostile or offensive, what is going to make a man feel sexually harassed by a woman? What kind of sexual behavior can intentionally or unintentionally make a man's working environment so uncomfortable that it interferes with his job?

- As with women, unwelcome sexual overtures or unwanted flirtation—particularly by a supervisor—can make a situation feel hostile. In addition to the same fears that women have about being coerced or punished by a boss, men worry that the situation will escalate to some version of the "Fatal Attraction" syndrome. They are afraid that if the woman feels spurned, she will undermine him, deliberately damage his reputation or even become overtly hostile.

- Men find male bashing and castration jokes offensive because these are unabashed expressions of female hostility toward men. This makes most men feel demeaned, disparaged and unfairly branded as a threat to women.

- Comments that reduce a man's behavior to stemming from sexual insecurity or the size of his penis are as offensive to men as remarks about PMS are to women. Insinuations that a man's actions are driven by testosterone are disparaging and dismissive—"Steve's brain is in his pants."

- Attempts by women to make men uncomfortable by, for example, swapping stories about labor and childbirth can also make men feel like they're being used as emotional punching bags. If you deliberately try to rattle someone, it's hostility, pure and simple. This is simply the female version of men trying to "gross out" women. Even if women don't set out to unsettle men by discussing reproductive or gynecological matters, continuing after realizing that a man is uncomfortable says that the women involved feel that a man's sensitivities need not be respected.

• Men find confronting a woman's sexual power on the job especially threatening. Observing a woman using her sexuality on the job—flirting, sweet talking or sleeping with a boss or colleagues—makes a man feel powerless by comparison. Men also worry about not alienating women who have "flirtatious friendships" with his superiors. A man knows that such a woman can ruin his career if she wants to.

For example, Karen had a flirtatious friendship with Tim's boss, and she tried to strike up the same thing with Tim. Tim found himself in a no-win quandary. Flirting on the job, even "just in fun," made him uncomfortable. However, because of how he had seen Karen behave at other times,

he was afraid that telling her this would lead her to say something negative about Tim to his boss. And at the same time, Tim worried that going along with Karen could make Tim's boss jealous. Tim felt himself to be in a threatening situation.

• Men are offended when women apply a double standard. It's not unusual for the same women who complain about men's commenting on women's bodies to make remarks about men's bodies. Women who object to "cheesecake" on the office walls may bring in "beefcake." Women may say, "Men have been doing it for years—what's good for the goose is good for the gander." But men consider the double standard to be hypocritical and aggressive.

• Mocking a man who complains about a woman's behavior or who alleges harassment is the ultimate double standard. Especially in light of all of the public discussion about the seriousness of men harassing women, men feel demeaned, insulted and discriminated against if their complaints are treated any less seriously than a woman's. Men feel they're being told that their complaint is suspect or unimportant because it comes from a man. That their feelings of being upset are being dismissed out of hand. Men who are ridiculed feel shamed and victimized by all of the old stereotypes: a "real man" should be able to take it; complaining shows that he's a baby; a man is obviously weak if he can let a woman unsettle or push him around; asking for someone to step in is like "running to Mommy"; if a man has a problem of this sort with a woman, it's because he selfishly and thoughtlessly misled her—so now it's time to take his medicine like a man.

What's the harm?

The ways that men can feel sexually harassed by women, then, are somewhat different from the ways women feel harassed by men. The threat of *quid pro quo* harassment and the obsessive actions of a sexually aggressive member of the opposite sex, of course, are equally threatening to both men and women. But most of what we've just looked at evokes feelings of powerlessness, anger or shame in men rather than, in the case of women, fear.

Nonetheless, the fact that being harassed may be a less intensely negative experience for men than for women is irrelevant. It does not change the fact that these emotions are disturbing in their own right. It does not change the fact that men are as entitled

as women to work in an environment that feels neither hostile nor offensive. And the behaviors that we've just considered can make a workplace feel uncomfortable for men. These behaviors definitely fit our opening definition of "sexual harassment."

Moreover, even if the experience of a hostile environment is less intense for a man, it still affects his job. Working in an environment in which you regularly feel that you're the target of someone else's aggression makes it harder to do your job. If men complain, they'll worry whether this will affect everything from how cooperative coworkers will be, to their chances for raises and promotions. Like women who have been harassed, men will change entrances, schedules, paths from one part of the company to another. In short, "hostile environment" harassment has the same affect on a man's job as it does on a woman's.

What to do?

As was the case with men harassing women, after we unravel the complexities involved in identifying and understanding the sexual harassment of men, there are few practical options for everyone involved.

- Women must accept the fact that men can be harassed. In particular, women must see how "male bashing" and applying a double standard make an environment feel hostile for men. Women must ask themselves, "If a man said about a woman what I just said about a man, would I be offended?"

- Men must recognize that most women have no idea that they make working environments feel as hostile for men as they do. Men must speak up. An uncomfortable situation will never change unless you say something. Also, be sure to explain what you're feeling and why: "Denise, whenever you and your friends start bashing men, I feel really uncomfortable. It feels like I'm being lumped in with all of the 'pigs' you complain about. That doesn't feel fair. And I don't like feeling like I'm the punching bag whenever you decide you're mad at the way men have treated women in the past."

Basaam and Judy

We can now return to our opening encounter between Basaam and Judy. And it should be apparent that there's no shortage of examples of what we've been talking about in this chapter.

Opening salvos

Both Basaam and Judy begin with aggressive potshots at the other. Given everything we now know about women's sensibilities, Basaam's greeting ("Excuse me, sweetcheeks, but you're in my seat") is bound to feel hostile to a woman sitting alone in an airport. Of course, Judy's insulting rejoinder ("You pig") and her lumping all men together ("You guys are all alike") is equally offensive to Basaam.

Unintentional harassment and different worlds

Judy recognizes that the men in her industry are probably not deliberately trying to give her a hard time. However, when it comes to hurting other people's feelings, intentions are largely irrelevant. The "virgin" imagery deeply offends Judy, whether it was intended to or not.

Judy's reaction and Basaam's observation that many men naturally talk that way point up the "different worlds" in which the sexes live. But because Judy's feelings about the comment are understandable in her world, Basaam's observation serves only to make matters worse. By dismissing Judy's reaction as "blowing this way out of proportion," Basaam revictimizes someone who's already been a victim. It doesn't matter that men call one another names with absolute equanimity. Women have very different sensibilities on this score. Basaam totally misses the seriousness of what Judy's just told him about her reaction.

The genuine article

Judy's story about Tony reveals that he is a genuine harasser. Grabbing a woman under the table in a business meeting to make her look bad is not *fun*; it's hostility. In addition, Harold's reaction to Judy's account reveals that he, too, is a hostile individual. As much as she'd probably like to let things ride, Judy has to speak to someone in her company about both Tony and Harold. She may be in a no-win situation. Her boss may be unsympathetic. But if she lets the situation continue, it will only get worse with both men.

Adding insult to injury

Basaam once again dismisses Judy's complaint. Even if Tony's a jerk, this is irrelevant and no defense for his threat. And, despite what Basaam says, in light of an ordinary woman's vulnerabilities, Harold's remark is a threat. In addition, Basaam's gratuitous "PMS" remark is offensive.

The double standard

Judy counters, however, with a remark equally offensive to Basaam because she uses a double standard. Despite the fact that Judy's just been looking for sympathy about being harassed, she now mocks the very idea that the same thing could happen to a man. This is as much a revictimization of Basaam as his dismissal of her troubles was. The fact that this episode caused Basaam to leave the company is testimony enough to how hostile the environment became for him.

Another genuine article

Basaam's account of Phyllis makes it plain that she's as much a genuine harasser as Tony and Harold. The key is that she continued to plague Basaam after he spoke to her. Basaam's description of the way he handled the situation also shows what little difference there is between the way men and women react. We all think that if we can just avoid a troublesome person, the problem will go away, and we won't have to confront this individual. However, this is not true if a genuinely aggressive person decides that you're his or her target. Unfortunately, what happened to Basaam shows how hanging back is always the wrong strategy. By letting things ride without informing someone in the company, Basaam left himself vulnerable to being misunderstood by his boss when things blew up.

Closing thoughts

Despite all of the attention that has been given to sexual harassment, this doubtless remains the most controversial aspect of how men and women relate in the workplace. As we've explained, dramatic differences in the experiences of each sex in our culture lead men and women to have very different ideas about what constitutes harassment. Moreover, despite the stereotype of the aggressive male, men and women alike are harassed by each other, only differently. As with everything we've discussed in this book, the key to dealing with these difficulties is appreciating just how different the "worlds" of other people are from our own, interpreting their actions accordingly, and communicating in a forthright fashion.

Chapter Six

It's all about safety and danger

By now you should have a basic grasp of the differences between warriors and villagers. You should be able to:

- Identify which you are.

- Identify the warriors and villagers around you at work.

- See some of the major problems that arise on the job as a result of the differences between warriors and villagers.

- Have some idea of how to avoid these difficulties.

- Have some idea of how to handle them if they arise.

But are you now more tolerant and accepting of those differences in your day-to-day dealings with other people? Probably not. Why? Because as the Buddha said (or at least should have said), "Warriors and villagers won't get along better in the office until they accept their differences in their hearts as well as they understand them in their heads."

More important than recognizing the differences between warriors and villagers is appreciating just how deep-seated these differences are, and understanding just why we all end up as one or the other. That's what will let you genuinely feel that warriors and villagers are both okay. Accepting the differences between one another is the key to smoothing things out in the workplace. Yet seeing how the differences between warriors and villagers spring from the realm of deep psychology is the key to understanding one another. And that's what we're going to work on in this final section.

Difficulties of dealing with each other

We believe that it's critical for all of us to accept in our hearts that it's okay that some of us are warriors and others villagers. If not, we'll just be going through the motions in trying to handle the differences between us. Especially in high-stress situations, we'll automatically revert to our normal way of doing things (and we'll wonder what's wrong with people different from us).

It's a fact of human psychology that it is genuinely difficult to accept profound differences between ourselves and others with equanimity. If we're honest, all of us would admit that we no doubt think that our way of thinking and acting is the best way. We all tolerate the fact that other people do things differently from us, but most of us don't really believe that another way of living really is as good as our own. We know all too well the strengths of our own approach to life and the weaknesses of other approaches. So the best that most of us can muster is a grudging tolerance for the fact that other people have a right to live by their "mistaken" choices.

However, if you want to learn how to deal more effectively with people different from yourself, it's critical to understand why each approach to life makes sense on its own terms.

Our awareness of the drawbacks of other people's ways of doing things usually surfaces as bias against people of the character type opposite us. This prejudice is, not surprisingly, completely unjustified and based on important misunderstandings between warriors and villagers. But, defensible or not, it's still there.

Before we can correct our own faulty attitudes, however, we first have to recognize them. So if we're going to get to the point of feeling that it's equally acceptable to be a warrior or villager, we first have to face some difficult facts about our own bias against people of the opposite type.

Warriors and villagers: our prejudices

If you're a warrior, you probably think that villagers are weak, frightened, gullible and insecure. You see a villager's obsession with relationships as emotional self-indulgence, and their cooperativeness as a spineless inability to stand up for themselves. Their concern with peace and harmony says to you that they are cowards with no stomach for a fight. You respect them less than warriors because you think that villagers ultimately have no respect for themselves. You see them as always making virtues out of their weaknesses.

What you find especially grating is how—behind your back—they talk about how superior they are to warriors, and how insensitive and uncivilized you are. You, of course, know that warriors are the superior ones, and that, at the great table of life, villagers deserve only the crumbs and leftovers that remain after warriors have had their fill. After all, whenever the village is in danger, the villagers' inferiority is made abundantly clear as they are forced to turn to the warriors to protect them.

If you're a villager, you no doubt share a corresponding intolerance. You see warriors as being arrogant savages. You find their fixation on winning as silly and childish. Furthermore, you consider their idea of success to be shallow and trivial. You see warriors as selfish brutes who have an immature disregard for other people. You see them as being profoundly insecure, emotionally stunted, and frightened by open and honest relationships. You see their delight in intimidating others as a mask that covers their inability to have equal relationships with other human beings. You have no patience for their huge egos, unending games and concern with protecting their turf. Their constant habit of putting their private interests before those of the group you find little short of criminal. And despite what warriors may say about a "code," you consider them to have no conscience whatsoever.

In short, villagers see warriors as essentially frightened children who work overtime at trying to conceal this fact from themselves. Villagers are certain that warriors will ultimately see the emptiness of their lives. And they take pleasure in the conviction that most warriors die filled with regret that they learned too late that the villagers were right all along about the path to happiness.

Setting things straight: it's all about feeling safe

It's hard enough for warriors and villagers to work well with each other

when we genuinely understand our differences, but it's virtually impossible if we're misreading each other and harboring ill will. So how do we get past these terrible biases against each other? What's the source of the misunderstanding? And how do warriors and villagers get to the point of sincerely respecting one another?

The secret is this. Ultimately, what we're talking about with warriors and villagers are differences at an unconscious level in what makes people feel safe. What determines whether we're warriors or villagers is what makes us feel secure or threatened. The most fundamental and most powerful psychological difference between warriors and villagers is that warriors and villagers have opposite ideas about what counts as safety and what counts as danger.

We guarantee that if you can honestly accept this core psychological difference between warriors and villagers, your prejudice and resentment will decrease. And you will have a much easier time handling the practical issues that come up in the workplace. You still may not like the differences between you and others, but you will be able to accept them better. And, despite yourself, you will probably begin to respect—even if grudgingly—people of the opposite type.

So how does this make us warriors or villagers?

So what's the link? How are differences in how we unconsciously perceive safety and danger connected to whether we're warriors or villagers?

The simplest way of putting this is as follows.

1. A central psychological fact about all of us is how we picture ourselves. When the world lets us live in a way that agrees with this picture of who we are, we feel safe and secure. But if the world makes it difficult for us to live according to this picture, we actually feel that we're in danger.

2. In the deepest reaches of their psyches, warriors picture themselves as solitary and independent individuals; the greatest threat to this autonomy is being under the control of other people. Villagers, by contrast, see themselves as being essentially connected to other people; it is separation from others that feels dangerous.

3. Thus, no matter what it looks like on the surface, warriors act like warriors in order to protect themselves from other people taking away their independence. Villagers act like villagers in order to avoid being alone in the world and having no one to rely on.

4. In other words, we're warriors or villagers because of what it takes for us to feel safe in the core of our souls.

Self, safety and danger

There is one thing that you absolutely, positively must take to heart in trying to understand the differences between warriors and villagers. And that's the idea that a critical psychological fact about all of us is a picture of ourselves that we carry around deep inside us. We might say that this self-image is so closely connected to whether we feel safe in the world that it's like our "psychological heart." If it's allowed to beat untroubled the way it's designed to, we feel healthy and safe. But if something gets in the way of its natural style of beating—if it has to struggle or strain, or if something throws off its rhythm—then we feel that our life is in danger. If the world around us puts roadblocks in the way of our living in line with our inner picture of ourselves, we don't just feel disgruntled or uncomfortable—we feel deeply threatened. So take the relationship between self-picture and feelings of safety and danger very seriously. This fundamental psychological fact will explain virtually everything that we said about warriors and villagers in this book.

As important as this matter is, however, it is also surprisingly uncomplicated. That's because it turns out that all of our self-pictures fall into one of only two categories: we see ourselves as either *separated* from other people or *connected* to other people. And that is the ultimate foundation of whether we are warriors or villagers.

Self-descriptions: separated and connected

Psychologists have discovered that when people are asked the question, "How would you describe yourself to yourself?," they respond in one of two ways. Either they answer something in the way that Mel does:

"I am of East Indian descent, relatively tall and thin. I have black hair and brown eyes. I have some artistic qualities and am handy in carpentry and auto mechanics. I possess relatively good mathematical ability and good judgment in business."

Or they respond more like Jennifer:

"I am a tall, friendly woman who enjoys being with friends and family. I am honest and loyal to people who treat me the same way. I am considerate of other people's feelings."

Each is a perfectly reasonable answer to the question, but notice the differences. Except for saying that she is tall and female, Jennifer cites traits that describe how she relates to other people. She is friendly, helpful, loyal, considerate and enjoys being with people she loves. Jennifer's description reveals that she sees herself as someone who is intimately connected with other people. The world in which she lives is essentially social because the traits she cites make sense only if there are other people with whom she can be friendly, helpful and loyal. These qualities also imply a strongly emotional character to these relationships.

Mel, on the other hand, cites physical traits and various skills that he possesses. These are all things to be proud of. But nothing about Mel's self-picture suggests that he has any significant contact with anyone else. It is quite possible to be an artistic or mathematically proficient carpenter with no one else around. Mel does refer to his ethnic heritage and to business—both of which imply other people. But Mel reveals little about the emotional character of his relationships with other people. Mel describes a largely independent and emotionally autonomous individual living in a very sparsely populated world.

If you ask warriors to describe themselves, you'll generally get a picture closer to Mel's. Villagers describe themselves more as Jennifer did. Thus, warriors ultimately see themselves as autonomous, independent and emotionally separated from others. Central to how villagers see themselves is being connected to other people.

Why the differences?

Mel's account of himself is as empty of people as Jennifer's is full of them, and it lacks the emotions that color Jennifer's self-description. Yet in reality, Mel is known by people close to him to be a man of strong feeling who is deeply attached to his family. So Mel's description really gives us only one side of him—the side separated from others. By the same token, Jennifer's portrayal of herself lacks important details that Mel's includes. She tells us little about who she is by herself, apart from other people. Jennifer is, in fact, a highly accomplished professional. So, like Mel, she too reveals only one side of herself—in her case, the side that's connected to others.

The point here is that each of them describes the side of themselves that they are most comfortable talking about (even if only to themselves). Or rather, to turn it around, they omit the part of their lives that in some way makes them uncomfortable. But why should they feel uneasy about describing the rest of their lives? The way the question is asked ("How would you describe yourself to yourself?") removes the issue of worrying about what other people will think about their answers. And it's not as though Mel and Jennifer are concealing something negative about themselves. What they don't reveal is decidedly positive. But psychologically, they're still uncomfortable doing so. Why? What's the source of the discomfort?

Warriors, other people, safety and danger

Recall that we've said that warriors like Mel have internal pictures of themselves as independent, solitary, free agents. Warriors ultimately feel most comfortable when they feel independent from other people and largely free from intense emotional entanglements with others. Independence and autonomy make them feel stronger. They enjoy the freedom of doing what they choose.

A sense of independence from others gives warriors "elbow room"—a psychological cushion. It probably even has a physical effect on warriors—making them feel more calm and probably even making it easier for them to breathe. But warriors don't merely feel comfortable when they feel independent. Being free and unfettered defines warriors so completely that they feel safe. That is, a sense of autonomy lets their "psychological heart" beat with ease.

But if independence feels safe, whatever threatens that autonomy must feel dangerous. And in a warrior's case, the main threat to their independence is other people. That is, other people— friends and foes alike—are the primary source of danger to a warrior's psychological security. Other people can overpower, control or harm a warrior.

Even good things can feel bad

Being under someone else's control is the greatest and the most obvious threat to a warrior's "psychological heart." But it's important to see that even positive connections with other people can threaten a warrior's sense of independence. For example, being in love—even when it is what a warrior consciously wants—can at times feel problematic. (This may not seem logical, but research in psychology suggests that it's true.) After all, intimacy and autonomy feel like opposite goals to a warrior. To encounter the emotional needs of another person can feel overwhelming. To admit that you depend on a single person to meet your deepest needs is to give that person considerable power over you. It makes warriors vulnerable to being hurt by their beloveds, and it also jeopardizes a warrior's sense of self-reliance.

Warriors feel safest when other people cannot harm them, that is, when competitors are under a warrior's power, or when friends and lovers can be kept at arm's length when necessary. Thus, warriors are driven to compete and to win in order to feel that potential enemies cannot hurt them. No matter what it looks like on the surface, warriors act like warriors because they're protecting themselves from other people taking away their independence or hurting them.

It's important to see, however, that because of the depth and power of the psychological forces involved, warriors themselves aren't consciously aware of the details of this process as it happens. Warriors simply do what comes naturally to them. They try to win. It doesn't feel to them as though they're trying to protect themselves because they're afraid of losing their sense of autonomy or being hurt. But that is in fact what's happening—even if it's mainly at an unconscious level.

And that's why Mel doesn't reveal his social side in his self-picture. The most logical reason for not populating your self-picture with other people is because, unconsciously, they represent some sort of threat. And as we've seen,

with warriors, that's precisely the case. So in the comfort of Mel's private account of himself, he relaxes, lets down his guard, and removes from his consciousness the primary source of danger in his life—other people.

Warriors and the pyramid

Another way of describing this is to say that warriors live in a world that is like a ladder or a pyramid. And they feel safest when they're at the top of the pyramid, with all of their adversaries below them.

Warriors are keenly aware of their position relative to other people. They know who is "above" them and who is "below" them, and they strive to move higher. Even in apparently trivial exchanges, they try to feel "on top." For example, when a group of warriors get together, they jostle for position. It may look like they're joking with or ribbing one another. But they're really trying to establish themselves as higher in a hierarchy. As we said, the psychological forces at play are so deep that most warriors don't recognize what's going on. They just do what feels comfortable. But competing and trying to win feels comfortable because, in a warrior's soul, it feels like the path to safety.

Villagers, other people, safety and danger

The story is just the opposite for Jennifer and other villagers. Psychologically, the basic image that villagers have of themselves is as part of a group. Their self-picture reveals that they feel that being connected to other people is positive, even nourishing.

As we saw with warriors, however, living in line with their self-picture doesn't simply let people feel comfortable, it makes them feel safe. Feeling connected to other people lets villagers feel that they are part of a group of people who care about one another and who will be there for each another in time of need. Strong, intense relationships make villagers feel secure and protected. Feeling close and connected to other people lets a villager's "psychological heart" beat comfortably.

But if close connections with others makes villagers feel safe, feeling separated from others must feel dangerous. Indeed, villagers seem to unconsciously believe that they cannot survive in the world unless they are part of a village. There seems to be a belief in the core of a villager's being that the more they are separated from other people, the more their life is in jeopardy. Separation from others, then, is what puts a strain on a villager's "psychological heart."

For villagers, being connected is so important that being separated from others is very unsettling—even painful. In fact, villagers live so much in a world filled with other people that losing this connection may even feel like losing a part of themselves. To be deprived of a feeling of safe and dependable emotional connections with other

people is enormously stressful for villagers. It would feel like being in the middle of a telephone conversation and for the lines to go dead. Or, at its worst, like being on a life support system and for the power to fail.

Even good things can feel bad

But, as we saw with warriors, seemingly positive things can register as dangerous in surprising ways. With villagers, anything that can threaten a sense of closeness with other people is problematic. For example, some psychological research suggests that villagers can feel unconsciously uneasy with professional success...things like making more money than other people, getting a major promotion, receiving unusual recognition, being placed in authority over other people. Villagers react this way because, even though villagers consciously want these things, they can distance villagers from one another. Being intimidating or superior to one another may make warriors feel safer in the world, but it makes villagers uneasy.

Villagers feel more kinship with villagers like themselves. Feelings of equality and similarity are the glue that keeps villagers together. This makes deep, mutual relationships easier. It also makes it more likely that villagers will develop the close feelings that will lead to a willingness to help each other. Seeming to be "better" weakens relationships with others, so villagers work very hard at playing down differences among themselves. Villagers who seem arrogant, self-important or self-reliant will more likely be shunned by other villagers in a time of crisis. Villagers fear that the more they're set apart from the group, the more they risk the ultimate danger...being abandoned by other villagers.

Villagers feel safest when they are connected to people around them who will help them. They feel safest when they relate to other villagers as equals and when these relationships are secure and dependable. Thus, villagers focus on developing close relationships with other villagers in order to increase the number of allies around them. No matter what it looks or feels like on the surface, villagers act like villagers in order to reduce the fear of being alone in the world and having no one to rely on.

And that's why Jennifer doesn't reveal her autonomous side in her self-picture. Like other villagers, central to who Jennifer is at the very core of her being is emotional relationships with other people, her involvement with their lives, and their involvement with hers. She minimizes the extent to which she can be seen as separated from other villagers because, unconsciously, this threatens her sense of safety in the world.

Villagers and the web

Another way of describing this is to say that villagers live in a world that is like a web. Each strand is a relationship with another villager. The more strands that make up the web, the stronger the web. The stronger each strand is, the safer the web. And the stronger the web is, the more secure villagers feel in life.

Villagers are thus experts in forging and strengthening relationships with other villagers. They are alert to both verbal and nonverbal cues about where they stand with other people. It is second nature for them to smooth the way to cooperative relationships with others because, in a villager's soul, this is what makes them feel safer.

The pyramid and the web: safety and danger

When we say that warriors and villagers live in "different worlds," we are referring to the differences between these images of life as a pyramid and life as a web. Life as a pyramid is life as a contest, with warriors battling to climb to the top. Life as a web is life as a community, with villagers working to forge strong connections with each other.

But notice that the "worlds" of warriors and villagers aren't just different, they're *opposite*. What counts as safety and danger are diametrically opposed in these two worlds. In the pyramid-like world of the warrior, other people are sources of danger. They threaten to dominate the warrior and take away the warrior's cherished autonomy. In the web-like world of the villager, however, other people are sources of safety.

Other people are allies, not adversaries. They are literally a "safety net."

Other people, safety, and danger

In terms of deep psychology, the single most important fact that defines warriors and villagers is how they regard other people. Living as they do in the middle of a battlefield, warriors see other people primarily as adversaries, that is, as sources of danger. Living in a close community, villagers see the people around them as friends and neighbors, that is, sources of safety. Warriors know that some other warriors can be allies, and villagers are aware that some villagers are untrustworthy, but their automatic reactions to other people are distrust and trust, respectively.

In their ordinary dealings with other people, warriors try to enhance their own power or status in order to decrease their unconscious fear of being dominated or hurt by others. Similarly, villagers try to develop equal and cooperative relationships in order to decrease the unconscious fear of being abandoned. It may not look like this on the surface. A warrior may act arrogant and self-serving. A villager may act weak and obsequious. In reality, they're both driven by opposite (and unconscious) ideas of how threatening other people are.

If you are skeptical, read this!

There's a good chance that some of you may be skeptical about this explanation of what determines whether we are warriors or villagers. You may find our claims about the unconscious and deep psychology unconvincing. You may reflect on your own feelings and dismiss what we've been saying about warriors and villagers having opposite, deep-seated ideas of safety and danger. Not everyone believes in the unconscious, or that it is as powerful as we suggest. But before you reject what we've been saying, we want you to consider one fascinating study that provides some backing for all of this.

Recall that at the beginning of this book, we explained that although we believe that sex is overstated as a cause of personality differences, we could not dismiss that gender might be a factor. Indeed, our description of warriors and villagers springs mainly from the body of research investigating differences between men and women. Accordingly, some of the gender research is very revealing about differences between warriors and villagers.

One particular study comes to mind. As a way of examining the idea that men and women perceive danger differently, two Harvard psychologists gave subjects a series of pictures and asked them to write stories describing what's going on. Two pictures showed people closely connected to one another (a man and a woman trapeze act, and a man and a woman sitting next to each other on a bench); two portrayed scenes of success or achievement (a man sitting at his desk in an office building, and two women working in a laboratory). The researchers discovered that the "connected" pictures were more likely to prompt the men in the study to write violent stories than the "achievement" stories, whereas it was the other way around for the women. The researchers reported that, "The content of the stories showed that the danger men saw in situations of affiliation was a danger of entrapment in relationships or of rejection or betrayal. In contrast, the danger that women described in situations of achievement was a danger of isolation, of being set apart and left alone." (*Journal of Personality and Social Psychology*, Vol. 42, No. 1, Susan Pollak and Carol Gilligan, "Images of Violence in Thematic Apperception Test Stories"). In other words, in line with what we've been saying about warriors and villagers, the men in the study perceived other people as dangerous, while the women saw danger in being separated from others.

What is significant about this study is that, like the "ink blots" that psychologists are so fond of, the pictures themselves are neutral. That is, there are absolutely no signs that anyone is in danger in the pictures. So if subjects write danger into a picture, it's because they're placing it there in response to the way that a picture stimulates them on a deep level. Psychologists call this process "projection" and claim that this reveals much about the nature of the inner world of the subjects. In this study, when men and women viewed

precisely the same pictures, men projected danger into pictures that put someone's autonomy at risk while women projected danger into pictures that put someone's connection at risk. And if the differences in the stories didn't come from differences in the men's and women's unconscious sense of safety and danger, it's hard to imagine where they did come from.

Warriors, villagers, safety and danger in real life

But how do these opposite senses of safety and danger play themselves out in real life? Consider the following examples.

....

Charlie had his own way of working. He had particular computer programs that he liked; particular tastes in the appearance of his presentations; and a particular willingness to spend any amount of time doing what most people considered cosmetic touchup. His productions were striking—and always late.

Everyone else in the office used the same software as each other, and they followed departmental guidelines regarding layout, formatting, graphics and the like. These guidelines were conservative, and resulted in unspectacular, but consistent documents. What the staff gained from their procedures was that they could exchange files. If one of them had done something similar to what another one needed to do, the second person could get a copy of the first person's file and fit it into his document easily. This ability to share work speeded up their work considerably. They were working as a team, producing usable documents quickly. Charlie had to work on his own; he could neither use other people's files, nor contribute to the pool.

Charlie does great work, but at a price. His "lone wolf" attitude has hurt the company's reputation. Missed deadlines caused two clients to cancel their orders. What's Charlie's problem? Nothing. He's a warrior, and he just feels safer working as he does. Charlie's confronted with a situation that can make him feel smothered. And for warriors, that's threatening. Keeping control over his own work, and working independently from the rest of the staff preserve his sense of autonomy. Indeed, a sure sign that something deep-seated is driving Charlie's behavior is that Charlie's willing to pay a price professionally—a reputation for always being late—just to do things his own way.

How could the situation be improved? Let Charlie continue to feel comfortable, but assign one person to act as liaison between Charlie and the rest of the team. (Charlie shouldn't find one person overwhelming.) Let that individual: keep Charlie posted on what the group is doing; keep the other people informed on what Charlie's doing; learn Charlie's software and procedures; and figure out how to convert his files into ones that could be used by the others. You might also consider asking Charlie to teach others his system. Charlie might begin to see other people's work as a resource that he could use when he decided to. And, by teaching, he should feel powerful and singled out. The trick is to preserve his sense of independence and control, while giving the rest of the staff enough access to his work so they could upgrade their own documents and help Charlie out in a bind.

....

Having enjoyed several good years in a row, the corporation that Eve worked for entered the recession over-staffed and over-diversified. The good times had led the company into a wide range of businesses, only a few of which the company knew anything about. And to operate these many businesses, the company employed a large number of people in an ever-growing bureaucracy.

The company was hard-hit by the sudden slowdown in sales that accompanied a static national economy. After much soul-searching, the senior managers of the company decided that they had to cut staff and get out of a number of businesses. They asked for recommendations for divestitures and layoffs from directors, including Eve.

Eve had a great number of friends in the organization. Those friends were in a variety of business lines. She called together the managers below her and asked them for ideas about where they could downsize the company. Each of them came back with a stirring defense of his or her area. When Eve tried to reach a consensus so that she could present a plan to her bosses, she ended up with nothing. She reported back to her bosses, saying that she thought that the company should try to hang tough during the hard times, keeping its people and lines of businesses intact. Because of Eve's reputation, senior management decided to delay implementing their original decision. During that time, the stock price fell, the economy got worse and the company's financial position deteriorated even more. Eve was not consulted when senior management began selling off divisions—at lower prices than they could have gotten originally—and letting more people go than they'd first planned.

Eve basically ignored what she'd been asked to do—offer suggestions for cuts. She misread the situation critically. What's wrong with her? Nothing. She's a villager, and feelings of danger got triggered. In Eve's case, the idea of cutting critical parts out of her "web" was so threatening that she couldn't bring herself to do it. She felt so closely connected to the people in the different parts of her organization that she lost perspective on what was really good for the business as a whole.

Suggestions? Someone has to help Eve see that if she is going to act effectively in such difficult situations, she has to rethink what will harm her "village." In reality, the fact that the situation felt

threatening enough to cloud her vision led to greater harm to people in the company than if she'd made the cuts originally. Villagers like Eve must come to see that their own fear of breaking connections and of firing people can sometimes be as much a threat to their web as any external threat.

....

Ben and Christy were their company's representatives at the important preliminary meeting with a major client. They had both worked on the material to be covered, and had an equal grasp of the project. Ben's assertive, blunt manner enabled him to communicate his ideas in a minimum number of words. He didn't bother to seek agreement from or understanding by most of the client's team. Rather, he pitched his conversation at the senior member of the team only. Christy talked more slowly, continually looked for signs of comprehension from the client's team, and encouraged questions and discussion.

Both Ben and Christy impressed their audiences. Realizing their different strengths, the company arranged that Ben would be the contact for the senior member of the client's team, while Christy would handle communications with all the others. Working in this way, they made a success of the project. The key was that they identified a strategy that utilized what each of them could do best.

This is an example of how warriors and villagers can be complementary in business. Ben's warrior sense of safety played itself out in his aligning himself only with the most powerful person on the client's team. Separating himself from the rest of the team was comfortable and protected him from feeling overwhelmed. Christy's villager need for safety, however, was met by developing connections with the very people Ben was distancing himself from. Although they hadn't planned it this way, the combination of their opposing styles let them accomplish something that neither could have done individually.

....

Remember, it's all about safety and danger

What you should now see is that what makes us warriors or villagers, and what shapes how we deal with each other is primarily a deep-seated sense of what counts as safety and danger. Warriors and villagers alike want to feel safe. And potential threats make them feel afraid, and prompt them to take defensive action.

So at this point, take a moment to think of all the times you've adopted a superior air and berated some warrior or villager. Now reinterpret their behavior in terms of what we've been saying about safety and danger. For example, the warriors you love to hate aren't aggressive and self-serving. They're in the middle of a battle and are afraid of being overwhelmed. Similarly, the villagers you can't stand aren't "kissing up" or trying to manipulate someone. They're alone at the edge of the village and are afraid of being without friends. What these people do that drives you crazy is really a defensive reaction to some threat in their world. It's not a "first strike" aimed at you.

If you can see things this way, your anger or disdain should begin to ebb. And you should begin to question the prejudices we listed at the start of this chapter. You should be able to see the opposite type as someone who lives in a different world than you do and, accordingly, has different sensibilities about safety and danger. You should be able to see that your own hostile reaction to them grows out of your own fears, that is, the way that their way of trying to feel safe triggers your own sense of danger. And once you get a handle on this, you should be able to understand your mutual fears and find some common ground on which to build a better way of dealing with each other.

And if all of this doesn't make you feel some genuine acceptance of all warriors and villagers as human beings worthy of your respect, go back and read this chapter again!

A
personal
note

We would like to end on a personal note, because in the course of writing this book, we had an interesting, illuminating and—we hate to admit—humbling experience that we found especially instructive in light of what this book is about.

· It's fair to say that after spending years researching the differences between warriors and villagers, teaching about them, conducting corporate workshops and talking to scores of people in business about them, we'd gotten pretty confident about all of this. We felt that we could easily recognize warriors and villagers around us, and we felt confident giving other people advice about how to handle problems that stemmed from the inevitable clash between these two ways of approaching the world. We understood these differences too well for them to spring any surprises on us—or so we thought.

In the early stages of writing, however, we ran into some significant problems working together—problems that we didn't bargain for and that greatly surprised us. We've known each other for years as colleagues and friends. The reason we decided to collaborate on this project in the first place is that we felt that we could easily work together and bring to the book our different experiences. However, our attempts to work out differences of opinion about the early chapters led to some tense exchanges and—if we're both really honest—resolutions never to collaborate with each other again.

What happened was this:

When we sat down to discuss each others' suggestions for improving the different sections that each of us had written in the early chapters, we kept running into roadblocks.

When Tom presented his criticisms of Katherine's work, she didn't agree with all of his ideas, but she graciously discussed them. When she began to suggest changes in Tom's portion, however, he took a different tack. For some surprising reason, Tom responded as though Katherine was telling him what to do, not simply making suggestions. Cooperation to him then felt like capitulation. He got annoyed, dug in his heels, and argued every point. After Katherine had been so cooperative in discussing his ideas, she was stunned by Tom's attitude. Katherine angrily called Tom on his reaction. And we were off to the races.

For reasons we still haven't figured out, in response to Katherine's suggestions, Tom "flipped" from villager to warrior. He then adopted the warrior belief that when you have a disagreement with someone, you don't give in, you fight it out. In villager mode, however, Katherine experienced Tom's "flip" to warrior as a personal attack. And, in self-defense, this led her to adopt a warrior stance as well.

What was so interesting about all of this, however, is that neither one of us recognized what was going on as it happened. These "flips" happened automatically and without warning. Each of us assumed that we were as cooperative and easygoing as always, and we wondered what was wrong with the other. Accordingly, we dramatically misread each other, interpreting professional suggestions as personal attacks. Fortunately, we both somehow felt that something was amiss, and we had the good sense to put things aside until we

could figure out some way to get the work done more productively.

As uncomfortable as it was to go through this, however, this experience did teach us some important lessons.

First, it reminded us that virtually all of us have both warrior and villager sides, even though our "shadow" side may rarely show itself. However, when you have a very strong personality, as each of us does, when your "shadow" side kicks in, it really kicks in.

Second, the fact that each of us can "flip" from villager to warrior or warrior to villager without warning, and without realizing it, impressed on us just how powerful our "shadow" sides are and how easily we settle into them.

Third, this experience taught us that no matter how well any of us intellectually understands the differences between warriors and villagers, we can all be blindsided by the psychological impact of these differences in real life when we least expect it. The fact that we were "experts" didn't protect us from the response that we both had when something in the exchange between the two of us registered unconsciously as a threatening experience.

And these are lessons that we hope you will take to heart as you look at how you relate to other people and how they relate to you on the job. Don't forget that you have both warrior and villager sides. Use this to your advantage when you can, in trying to be more effective in your dealings with others. But be on the lookout as well for your "other side" surfacing when it's not in your interest. At the same time, don't forget that everyone else also has their "shadow" side. So if they start acting out of form, don't ask what's *wrong* with them. Ask yourself whether they've somehow responded to a threat in their environment and "flipped" over to the other character type as a way of protecting themselves.

We can say from personal experience that understanding what's really going on will *definitely* help you get through times like this.

In case you're interested

If you'd like to learn more about the differences we've been describing, here are some readings you can look at.

Fire in the Belly: On Being a Man, Sam Keen (Bantam Books) and *The Male Ego,* Willard Gaylin (Penguin Books). These two books illustrate how the "warrior" has become a common image in the literature of the men's movement.

Men Are From Mars, Women Are From Venus. John Gray (HarperCollins Publishers, Inc.). The title of this bestseller says it all! Psychologist Gray describes fundamental emotional differences between men and women and how they surface in personal relationships.

You Just Don't Understand: Women and Men in Conversation. Deborah Tannen (William Morrow and Company, Inc.). Tannen is a sociolinguist at Georgetown University whose bestseller explores differences in the way that men and women communicate with each other.

In a Different Voice: Psychological Theory and Women's Development. Carol Gilligan (Harvard University Press). Gilligan is a moral development psychologist at Harvard whose landmark book argues that the majority of men and women approach and resolve ethical dilemmas differently. Gilligan claims that men are most comfortable thinking about right and wrong with a hierarchical-based "ethic of justice" (originally described by psychologist Lawrence Kohlberg), while women tend to use a relationship-based "ethic of care."

"Images of Violence in Thematic Apperception Test Stories," *Journal of Personality and Social Psychology,* Susan Pollak and Carol Gilligan, 1982, Vol. 42, No. 1. This is the study referred to in Chapter 6 about differences in how men and women perceive danger.

Various management specialists have claimed that there are important differences in how men and women operate in business. Sally Helgesen contrasts a male preference for "hierarchy" with a female preference for a "web" of relationships in *The Female Advantage: Women's Ways of Leadership* (Doubleday).

In her book, *Feminine Leadership, or How to Succeed in Business Without Being One of the Boys* (Times Books), Marilyn Loden argues that men in business are most comfortable with a competitive, high-control style of management aimed at winning. Women, she says, prefer a more cooperative, low-control, collaborative approach aimed at quality output.

In "Ways Women Lead" (*Harvard Business Review*, November-December 1990), Judy Rosener writes that most men manage through a "command-and-control" leadership style, while most women prefer an "interactive and participative" style.

Men and Women at Work